HANNAH MO

£2

Educational pioneer, playwright, social reformer,
evangelical Christian Hannah More was right at the
hub of the vivid cultural, political and religious life in
the England of 1800.

She had a talent for friendships, and their scope
was wide: Dr Samuel Johnson, colossus of the world
of letters; David Garrick, the most celebrated actor
of his time; William Wilberforce, who led the fight
against slavery; hymnwriter John Newton. . . She was
close to the 'Clapham Sect' of influential Christians,
and a member of the Bluestocking Club, in the van-
guard of women's arrival on the literary scene.

Hannah More's plays saw considerable success on
the London stage. And she was one of the first to see
the need for schools to reach all levels of society:
the More schools in the Mendip mining villages of
England's west country were educationally ahead of
their time.

JEREMY AND MARGARET COLLINGWOOD live in Bristol,
Hannah More's home city. Margaret is a freelance
broadcaster with the BBC and deputy editor of *The
Clifton Digest*. Jeremy, a student of Bristol's local
history, is vicar of Hotwells, the parish where Hannah
More lived until her death.

This is the first biography of Hannah More for
nearly forty years.

To our daughters,
Olivia, Elizabeth and Emma.

Hannah More

Jeremy and Margaret Collingwood

A LION PAPERBACK

Oxford · Batavia · Sydney

Copyright © 1990 Jeremy and Margaret Collingwood

Published by
Lion Publishing plc
Sandy Lane West, Littlemore, Oxford, England
ISBN 0 7459 1532 9
Lion Publishing Corporation
1705 Hubbard Avenue, Batavia, Illinios 60510, USA
ISBN 0 7459 1532 9
Albatross Books Pty Ltd
PO Box 320, Sutherland, NSW 2232, Australia
ISBN 0 7324 0221 2

First edition 1990

British Library Cataloguing in Publication Data
Collingwood, Jeremy
  Hannah More.
  1. Christian church. Evangelism. More, Hannah, 1745–1833
  I. Title   II. Collingwood, Margaret
  269.2092

  ISBN 0–7459–1532–9

Typeset by Selectmove Ltd, London
Printed and Bound in Great Britain
by Cox and Wyman Ltd, Reading

CONTENTS

1	The Darling Child	7
2	The Young Schoolmistress	15
3	The Jilted Bride	23
4	The London Celebrity	31
5	The Blue Stocking	41
6	The Fledgling Evangelical	55
7	The Noble Patron	63
8	The Indignant Abolitionist	67
9	The Mendip Reformer	73
10	The Greater Schools	79
11	The Lesser Schools	89
12	The Reluctant Controversialist	95
13	The Christian Moralist	101
14	The Popular Propagandist	111
15	The Spiritual Writer	119
16	The Honoured Philanthropist	133
17	The Happy Saint	143
	Notes to the Text	149
	Index	158

1
THE DARLING CHILD

The intelligent child perceives his father's motive
in restraining him, till . . . he loves the father
the more for the restraint; on the other hand,
the mismanaged and ruined son learns
to despise the father.

Christian Morals

The bells pealed out joyfully at Clifton Parish Church in Bristol. It was the wedding day of the beautiful Miss Hannah More. Her four sisters waited excitedly at the church, for she was the first of the five girls to be married, and her bridegroom, the squire of Belmont House, Mr Edward Turner, was considered quite a catch.

They waited in vain. Word came from Belmont that Mr Turner wished to postpone the wedding. It was once too often for Hannah, who had already put up with two postponements. The five sisters could only return home disconsolate, and resume their busy lives. Hannah, the adored sister around whom the others revolved, was not now destined to be mistress of a Somerset estate, and a new role had to be found for her.

Instead of quiet domesticity, in obscurity, Hannah was to blaze a trail for women. By her own pen she earned a fortune, using it to set up a cottage industry producing moral tracts that sold in their millions in Britain, America and other parts of the English-speaking world. Through her pioneer work in the schools in the Mendip Hills near Bristol, she set in motion a whole new programme of popular education, and gave literacy and dignity to thousands of poor children. Adored by men, she flirted with some of the most distinguished of her time, including Dr Johnson, David Garrick, Sir Joshua Reynolds and Horace Walpole, but chose to remain single. She mixed with the London intellectual set and became a member of the exclusive women's movement, the Blue Stockings. Success fell into her lap. People flocked to her plays and bought her books. Bishops and politicians sought her advice and counsel.

Yet throughout her life of fame and fortune Hannah never lost her innocence and charm nor swerved from her religious convictions. She became the confidante of the powerful, and advised princesses, but was also a friend to the poor. She was at heart a teacher, and remained so to the end of her days. Her classroom grew beyond her school in Bristol's Park Street to the drawing-rooms of London society and the hovels of the rural poor. Born and bred in a school, she felt it her responsibility to educate and inform all she met in the liveliest ways she knew, whether about moral living, abolishing the slave trade, preventing a revolution or getting a fair deal for the poor. It made no difference to her whether her pupils were the scruffiest and poorest children of Mendip miners or the leaders of society. To each she gave herself without reserve.

Hannah became one of the major driving forces in teaching the nation to read. Apart from the Bible there was little written for the popular market, but she rose to the challenge of providing edifying and compelling stories. Soon nearly every cottage in England had at least one of her Cheap Repository Tracts. It is impossible to calculate precisely what effect this nearly forgotten woman had on the minds of the British people in succeeding generations. But there can be little doubt that her writings, which reached into the homes of prince, prelate and pauper, helped to shape the thinking and the behaviour of Victorian England.

What was it in Hannah's character that enabled her to turn her humiliating rejection at the altar into such creative and practical activity? The Mores came from solid East Anglian Puritan stock. Her father, Jacob More, had two uncles who were captains in Oliver Cromwell's army during the English Civil Wars (1642-51). Jacob's mother was a remarkable woman who learned to bleed herself rather than call out the doctor. A staunch Presbyterian, she always rose at four even during the winter and lived to the age of ninety. In her youth Presbyterian worship was forbidden, but secret services were held in the house in the middle of the night with Hannah's great-grandfather guarding the house with a drawn sword.

Hannah's father was not a Presbyterian like his mother but a high Tory and Anglican, and it was in this tradition that he brought up his family. Born around 1700 at Thorpe Hall, Harleston, near Bungay in Norfolk, he was educated at Norwich Grammar School and had intended to take Holy Orders. He also hoped to inherit an estate at Wenhasten worth more than eight thousand pounds a year, a considerable fortune for those days, but lost his claim to a cousin. Denied this inheritance and the financial means to be ordained, Jacob moved to the West Country to start afresh. Unfortunately, most of the books he owned were lost at sea in a storm while being transported round the coast to his new home. Jacob lived for a time at Gloucester before moving to Bristol where he obtained a post as a supervisor of excise.

Through the patronage of the local landowner, Norborne Berkeley of Stoke Park, Jacob More was appointed to the school at Fishponds. Fishponds was then a hamlet in the parish of Stapleton on the outskirts of Bristol. This was a charity school endowed by the Berkeley family and others to provide free education for local children. The pupils were schooled in the four Rs of Religion, Reading, Writing and Arithmetic. Some Latin and craftwork were also taught. When they left school the boys were apprenticed to local craftsmen and traders. Norborne Berkeley became Baron Bottetourt in 1764 and went on to be Governor of Virginia. Later the Berkeley family were to play pivotal roles in the Hannah More story.

It was at Fishponds that Jacob More met and married Mary Grace, the daughter of a farmer from the nearby village of Stoke. William Roberts, Hannah's first biographer, says that Jacob 'married a young woman of plain education, the daughter of a creditable farmer, but endowed, like himself, with a vigorous intellect'.[1] The Grace family do not feature much in the journals of the More sisters, who may have felt that Jacob had married somewhat beneath himself. Even so, members of the Grace family were generously remembered in the wills of Hannah and her sister Martha. We know very little of Hannah's mother, Mary, although she seems to have been a woman of strong character. Mary bore Jacob five children, all daughters. Hannah, the fourth child, was born on 2 February 1745 in the schoolhouse in Manor Road, Fishponds.

Jacob was a well-educated man, widely read and a greatly respected teacher. He passed on all he knew to his children. They in their turn were to teach others. This was a time when young girls were only just being allowed into the classroom. The rich had governesses; the rest had nothing. There was an educational vacuum to be filled, but it was nonetheless most unusual for the

More girls as mere teenagers to set up their own select school for young girls.

Hannah was a precocious child. Her nurse, who had lived in the house of the poet Dryden, was soon being pumped for stories about him. Her mother had taught her to read at the age of three. By the ripe old age of four she recited her catechism in the parish church and had written these lines about the road past her home:

This road leads to a great city,
Which is more populous than witty.[2]

Hannah as a young child would keep whatever scraps of paper she could get hold of on which to scribble some story or poem. She would hide these efforts in the broom cupboard. Sometimes at night Martha would tiptoe downstairs to get a light so that Hannah could write down her compositions. She much enjoyed writing imaginary letters seeking to reclaim depraved men and women from the error of their ways, and then following them with fictitious responses full of appreciation and good resolutions. Hannah's mother recounted that one of Hannah's childhood games was to pretend that her chair was a carriage and to invite her sisters to join her to ride to London to see bishops and booksellers.

Jacob More had lost his library, and had no funds to replace it, but he had a marvellous memory. He used to tell stories to Hannah while she sat on his knee, stories of classical heroes first in Latin or Greek and then in English. Hannah, despite ill health, was something of a child prodigy, and soon outstripped Jacob's boy pupils at his school in Fishponds. He taught her Latin and mathematics until he grew alarmed by her ability, for he shared the popular notion of the time that the female brain was more delicate than the male and could be damaged by too much book learning at an early age. So the maths lessons were suspended. But Hannah's mother was keen that her promising daughter should receive the fullest education. Together they badgered Jacob to allow Hannah to continue her studies in other areas.

Hannah probably gained whatever poetic skills she possessed from her father, who enjoyed writing poetry throughout his life. In 1781, she wrote home to thank her father for his verses written at the age of eighty-one. She doubted whether she would write such verses at his age. Hannah was fortunate to have enjoyed such a good relationship with her father.

Years later, when writing about the Lord's Prayer, she could say:

> *Of all the compellations by which the Supreme Being is designated in his Holy Word, there is not one so soothing, so attractive, so interesting, as that of Father . . . It fills the mind with every image that is touching, and the heart with every feeling that is affectionate. It inspires fear softened by love, and exhibits authority mitigated by tenderness.[3]*

As fourth in line Hannah had the advantage of older sisters to learn from, and a younger sister she could perform to and take care of. Perhaps her younger sister was her favourite. Patty — her real name was Martha but they all used her nickname — was her audience as Hannah invented stories and delighted in telling them aloud. They loved to play-act together, and poor Patty even had to sit through Hannah preaching play sermons from a mock pulpit! It was from her eldest sister, Mary, that Hannah learned French. Mary was sent to a French school in Bristol and, as part of this privilege, was expected to teach her sisters the lessons that she had learned each week.

Hannah had a happy childhood, surrounded by love. She would need this stable background to cope with the flattery as well as the vilification she would meet in response to her work and writings. At home she was always the charmer, the performer who loved to hold centre stage. Her sisters gladly yielded this to her. There was only twelve years' difference between Mary, the eldest, and Patty, the youngest. Mary was the responsible older sister, blunt and bossy. She took charge of things and was later called 'the Man of the Family'. Next came Elizabeth, or Betty. Gentle and domesticated, 'the Good Angel', the cook and craftworker, she was 'the Wife of the Family'. Sarah, or Sally, the middle sister, was the wag and wit. She delighted in shocking others with her indiscretions. She wrote a couple of anonymous novels which, sadly, have not survived.

After Hannah came Patty, the youngest. She has been described as Hannah's slave and tyrant. She was strong willed but intensely loyal to Hannah. With her quick wit and vibrant humour she made an excellent companion for Hannah's later excursions into London society. It is from Patty's journal *Mendip Annals* that we learn about the daring adventures of these two in places where even law enforcement officers dared not go, as they opened up schools for the deprived and impoverished in Somerset.

The girls lived in the school house at Fishponds. The gaunt stone house is still standing, undistinguished apart from a plaque to Hannah. Today that road Hannah wrote about is busy night and day, often congested with traffic. Nearby is Manor Park Hospital, which in Hannah's childhood housed French officers held prisoner during the Seven Years War of 1756-63. Jacob More in his large-hearted fashion often invited them to his home. A spin-off from his hospitality was that Hannah learned to speak a colloquial French, something her sister could not have taught her.

The girls were fortunate to have a father who considered their education so important. For example, when the sisters moved right into Bristol and Mary opened her own school, Hannah had lessons from the classical tutor at Bristol Baptist Academy. The tutor, James Newton, said that, although Hannah studied with him for only ten months, she surpassed any other students he had ever had. There was no thought or question of Hannah going on to university, or even to school for higher education. No British university offered places to women until the founding of London University in 1836. Instead Hannah joined Mary's staff and became a pupil teacher, widening her education however she could. Visiting lecturers came to Bath and Hannah took every opportunity to hear them, so learning something more of literature, astronomy, elocution, religion, philosophy and science.

Hannah lived to see the fulfilment of her childhood ambitions. She did not seek husband and children, a good marriage or wealth. She wanted to live in a cottage 'too low for a clock' and to go to London to see bishops and booksellers. Both these dreams were to be realized. Hannah had a cottage built for herself at Cowslip Green in Somerset. We do not know whether she had a clock, grandfather or otherwise, in her first home, but the ceilings were low. She not only met bishops but corresponded with the great men of religion of her day, among them John Newton and John Wesley. She associated with members of the Clapham Sect, a wealthy group of prominent evangelicals, who campaigned for the abolition of slavery, the extension of education and other measures of social improvement. Her Cheap Repository Tracts were the start of the Religious Tract Society established to promote popular and cheap religious literature. Her stand on religious issues was so strong that William Cobbett derisively called her the 'Old

Bishop in Petticoats'. And booksellers were only too delighted to meet her — editions of her works were sometimes sold out soon after they were printed.

With no husband, and no dowry, how did she become so successful?

2
THE YOUNG SCHOOLMISTRESS

The great uses of study to a woman
are to enable her to regulate her own mind,
and to be instrumental to the good of others.

Strictures on Female Education

'On Monday after Easter will be opened a school for young ladies by Mary More and sisters, where will be carefully taught French, Reading, Writing, Arithmetic and Needlework.' This announcement in a Bristol paper on 11 March 1758 was repeated the following week with the additional statement: 'A dancing master will properly attend.'[1]

The More sisters began to make their mark on the world by establishing a girls' school. This started initially at 6 Trinity Street, close to St Augustine's Church and Bristol Cathedral. Sally More later told Dr Johnson how it all started. She described

> *how we were born with more desires than guineas, and*
> *as the years increased our appetites, the cupboard at home began to*
> *grow too small to gratify them: and how, with a bottle*
> *of water, a bed and a blanket, we set out to seek our fortunes: and*
> *how we found a great house with nothing in it, and*
> *how it was like to remain so till, looking into our knowledge-boxes,*
> *we happened to find a little* larning *. . . and so, at last, by giving*
> *a little of this little* larning *to those who had less, we got a good*
> *store of gold in return but how, alas, we wanted the wit to keep it.*[2]

So the More school for young ladies opened with Mary, then aged nineteen, as principal, and Betty, seventeen years, as housekeeper.

Sally, Hannah and Patty started as pupils but in due course were promoted to under-governesses. The sisters had no capital of their own but raised funds by subscription. Wealthy local families acted as patrons of the school. Among them were Mrs Edward Gwatkin from the Lovell family and, with her brother, a co-heir of the family estate at Trefusis in Cornwall. It is probable that other subscribers included Jacob More's old patron Norborne Berkeley of Stoke Park and his sister Elizabeth, who was the Dowager Duchess of Beaufort, and possibly Mrs Boscawen, widow of the Admiral and related by marriage to the Beauforts.

With the aid of various assistants the sisters provided a sound education for the daughters of an increasingly prosperous merchant class. Until the Industrial Revolution Bristol was the second city in England after London. It was connected by a good road to London, and the British Flying Machine, as the coach was called, made the trip three times a week in the summer months. The 120-mile journey to London then took two days. Bristol's prosperity was built on maritime trade with Russia and the Baltic in timber and furs, and on the lucrative profits of the triangular trade with Africa and the West Indies. English manufactures were carried to the West Coast of Africa where they were traded for slaves. The slaves were shipped across the Atlantic to the West Indies or the American colonies. There the English ships loaded sugar, rum and tobacco for the home run to Bristol.

After four years the More sisters moved their school from Trinity Street to a newly built house at 43 Park Street, now a fashionable shopping street running down towards the Cathedral. There the school remained under the control of the Mores until 1790. Mrs Elizabeth Montagu, one of the great ladies of London society, praised the sisters for the management of the school: 'They are all women of admirable sense and unaffected behaviour and I should prefer their school to any that I have seen for girls whether very young or misses in their teens.'[3]

The school in Park Street held as many as sixty girls and their teachers. We can picture them dressed in ballooning skirts with tightly corseted waists processing in double file down Park Street on their way to church. The girls would have been carefully chaperoned, since there was no lack of adventurers willing to take advantage of young girls who were both innocent and rich. After the More sisters sold the school there was a *cause célèbre* involving a West Indian heiress, Clementina Clerke, who was abducted to

Gretna Green by a Bristol chemist, Richard Perry. Gretna Green was where English couples could use the law of Scotland to get married without parental consent. Perry escaped from his pursuers in Chester by pulling a pistol on them and fled to London. Hannah More took part in a vain search of London boarding houses for the couple. Perry was eventually brought to trial but was acquitted. He later deserted Clementina and lived grandly in Jamaica on the estate acquired from her by marriage.

In addition to a general arts education, the girls received instruction in dancing and music. Mary Alden Hopkins, the American biographer of Hannah, obtained the bill in Hannah's handwriting for the education of one girl, Martha Lintorn, for the period June to December 1776. This shows that in addition to the cost of tuition, board, dancing and music amounting to £20. 7s. 0d., there were further expenses of £21. 8s. 10d. for the stay-maker, the linen-draper, the milliner, the shoe-maker, the robe-maker and the mercer. Included also was the sum of 8s. for two tickets for a play.[4]

Hannah went to no college to learn how to be a teacher. She learned her trade on the job, graduating by degrees from student teacher to teacher. Marianne and Tom Macaulay later testified to her natural abilities with young children. She was warm and friendly with her pupils. She wrote nursery rhymes and fairy tales for them, and told them the 'Bible stories of Joseph and his brothers and the wonderful adventures of the Children of Israel with such eloquence and force that I fancied she must have lived among them herself'.[5] In place of the fearful system of learning by rote, Hannah sought to hold the attention of the children by stimulating their imagination and using drama wherever she could. Her aim, she said, was to show 'Christ walking on the water not of Genessaret but Thames'. It was in the Park Street School that Hannah sharpened her didactic skill. Education was to be her driving instinct not only when teaching the children of Mendip, but later when she took it upon herself to be the instructor of the nation through her writings.

Hannah took particular pleasure in taking her girls to the theatre. Her introduction to the theatre came through a school parent, the actor William Powell. Hannah wrote the prologue to *Hamlet* spoken by Powell in one of his benefit nights at the old Jacob's Wells Theatre in Hotwells, Bristol. William Powell became actor-manager at the Theatre Royal, which opened in King's Street, Bristol, in 1776, but died suddenly after only three years in the job. His early death was attributed to his throwing himself naked into cool green grass after being overheated from a game of tennis. Hannah was devoted to Powell and took turns with Mrs Powell at his bedside. He died in Hannah's arms.

After Powell's death Hannah took her girls to see John Palmers' company, a father and son team, who brought their troupe over weekly from the Orchard Theatre in Bath to the Theatre Royal in Bristol. Bath was still the principal attraction for fashionable society, but Bristol opened up its own watering place at Hotwells, near the Park Street school, and the place where Hannah spent her last years. There the leisured classes could drink the waters from the St Vincent Rocks hot springs, and attend the assemblies on Mondays and Thursdays. These were presided over by a master of ceremonies with ribbon and medallion enforcing the rules of etiquette as prescribed at the Bath Assembly Room.

Hannah early on turned her hand to occasional verse. She wrote an epitaph for Fortune Little in St Mary Redcliffe Church. Her first ode was prompted by a lecture on rhetoric delivered by Thomas Sheridan, father of the dramatist Richard Sheridan. Thomas belonged to the old ranting school of actors and was known as 'Old Bubble and Squeak'. But Hannah was much moved by Thomas' dramatic renditions and wrote a poem in his praise. Thomas introduced Hannah to his delightful wife, Frances, who was both a playwright and novelist, and later to his son Richard and his daughter-in-law, the lovely singer Elizabeth Linley.

In school Hannah used drama to teach Bible stories. She wrote a number of *Sacred Dramas* which were performed by the girls before they were eventually published in 1782. But despite the religious subject matter, the public did not always approve of biblical theatre in those days. In Hull the attempt to put the *Sacred Dramas* on the stage hit local headlines when it incurred hostility from some 'religious' people. The Bible was thought to be appropriate only in church and not in the theatre. Yet *Sacred Dramas* ran into nineteen editions and was translated into Sinhalese. When only sixteen Hannah wrote a play entitled *The Search after Happiness* in which a party of young ladies weary of themselves and the world consult Urania, a worthy shepherdess, who sends them away greatly edified. Hannah herself described the play as 'void of wit and free from love'. This was no doubt why it commended itself to teachers and parents who were highly suspicious of anything theatrical which might lead pupils and daughters away from the high road of virtue and chastity. *The*

Search after Happiness ran into nine editions and sold over ten thousand copies.

Here is a sample of the play where Hannah seeks to reassure the audience that the girls are not to be corrupted by education but will remain good housewives and mothers. At the same time she is cocking a subtle snook at the chauvinistic assumptions that girls were incapable of learning and writing.

Second Young Lady:
Child! we must quit these visionary scenes,
And end our follies when we end our teens,
These bagatelles we must relinquish now,
And good matronic gentlewomen grow;
Fancy no more on airy wings shall rise,
We must scold the maids and make the pies;
Verse is a folly — we must rise above it,
Yet I know not how it is — I love it.
Tho' should we still the rhyming trade pursue,
The men will shun us, — and the women too;
The men, poor souls! of scholars are afraid,
We shou'd not, did they govern learn to read,
At least in no abstruser volume look,
Than the learn'd records — of a Cookery book;
The ladies, too, their well-meant censure give,
'What! — does she write? a slattern, as I live —
'I wish she'd leave her books, and mend her cloaths,
'I thank my stars I know not verse from prose;
'How well these learn'd ladies write,
'They seldom act the virtues they recite;
'No useful qualities adorn their lives,
'They make sad Mothers, and still sadder Wives.'

The Mores' next-door neighbour in Park Street was Dr (afterwards Sir James) Stonehouse, a clergyman who had at one time been in medical practice in Northampton. He had formerly been a Deist but had since become an Evangelical. The Deists were rationalists whose God was a remote deity who had created the world as a clock-maker who makes a clock, winds it up, and then leaves it to run its course. The Evangelicals, by contrast, taught that God could be known personally through faith in Jesus Christ. They laid much emphasis on the Bible as the sure Word of God and the divine rule

19

in matters of faith and practice. Dr Stonehouse was Rector of Great and Little Cheverell in Wiltshire, and also held a lectureship at All Saints in Bristol. Stonehouse was wealthy, well-connected and an eloquent preacher. He became a good friend of the Mores, whom he referred to as the Sisterhood. Dr Stonehouse recognized Hannah's exceptional gifts, and was full of praise for her liveliness and fertile imagination in conversation. Hannah said that Dr Stonehouse 'first awakened me to some sense of serious things'; and he guided her in her religious reading. It was Hannah who wrote the epitaphs for Sir James Stonehouse and his wife in Dowry Chapel, Hotwells.

Another spiritual mentor at this time was Josiah Tucker, the Rector of St Stephen's in Bristol, and later Dean of Gloucester. Tucker is known principally as a political economist but, according to the then Bishop of Bristol, Thomas Newton, he was 'a pattern parish priest'. It is not known for certain if the More sisters met the Wesleys in Bristol. John Wesley had opened his New Room, the first Methodist meeting house, in Bristol in 1739. He often stayed in rooms above the church (which can still be seen today) and made it the base for his missionary travels around England and Wales. In 1790 John declined an invitation to meet the More sisters on the grounds of other commitments and doubting whether his conversation would suit them.[6] His brother, Charles, the hymn writer, also lived in Bristol from 1752 to 1772. When Charles Wesley was an old man, Hannah introduced him in Bath to her young friend, William Wilberforce, the campaigner against the slave trade.

Bristol in those days was not the cultural backwater that London society may have imagined. After all the boy poet, Thomas Chatterton (1752-70), came from Redcliffe in Bristol where his father, like Hannah's, was the schoolmaster. Chatterton wrote poetry under the pseudonym of a fifteenth-century Bristol monk, Thomas Rowley, a fictitious character created by Chatterton. Fame came to Chatterton only after his premature death at seventeen from arsenic poisoning and starvation in a London garret in Holborn. The Mores knew the Chatterton family and were kind to the poet's mother after his untimely death. Later Ann, the boy's sister, lived with the More sisters at Barley Wood.

Hannah's talents enabled her to move easily among other literary figures in Bristol. There was Samuel Peach, a wealthy and learned linen draper, with a shop in Maryleport Street. Peach was friendly with the famous Scottish philosopher David Hume, who had worked for several years in a Bristol counting house, and had edited some of his work. Hannah met John Ford, founder of the Bristol Literary Society, and Amos Cottle, the bookseller and poet, whose two daughters attended the More school. She also formed a close friendship with James Ferguson, the popular astronomer, who was giving some lectures in Bristol. He is said to have been so impressed with her good judgment that he let her look over most of his writings before publication. But perhaps the most important of all those who came to 43 Park Street was the local Member of Parliament, Edmund Burke.

Burke, a distinguished parliamentarian, was both a prominent political thinker and a great orator. He was strongly opposed to George III's attempts to assert a more active role for the Crown and forcefully argued for the independence of MPs as free representatives and not delegates. He proposed conciliatory policies towards the American colonies and Ireland. But the excesses of the French Revolution so horrified Burke that his thinking later became more conservative, and he opposed changes in the constitution which might upset the established rights and privileges of the ruling classes. There can be little doubt that Hannah, who became a close admirer and supporter of 'the sublime and beautiful' Burke, was greatly influenced by his thinking.

There was great excitement in the Park Street School at the general election in 1774. Edmund Burke rushed down from Yorkshire in his chaise, covering the 274 miles in forty-four hours, no mean feat for those days. On arrival in Bristol he went straight to the Guildhall where he delivered a very effective speech. After the declaration of the vote the excited election party gathered outside 43 Park Street and gave three cheers for the winning candidates. Hannah, who had written verses in support of Burke, was acclaimed by the literary-minded crowd as Sappho, the great lyric poet of ancient Greece. The More sisters celebrated Burke's victory by making a cockade, or rosette, for his hat. This was entwined with myrtle, ivy, laurel and bay, and decorated with silver tassels. They also presented him with a wreath and some of Hannah's fulsome verse. Burke wore this cockade as he was chaired around the city. Later he called at the house to thank the sisters and to pay them charming compliments. Edmund and his brother Richard became frequent visitors to the More household. All these contacts were to be invaluable when Hannah was to make her way to London in search of bishops and booksellers.

21

3
THE JILTED BRIDE

Many a young woman, who would be
shocked at the imputation of an intrigue,
is extremely flattered at the idea
of a sentimental connection.

Essays

Hannah More enjoyed the company of men. She was unafraid
to converse with them on equal terms and impress them with
her intelligence and charm. She never seemed to lack men who
swarmed around her as bees around their queen, for she was
undoubtedly an attractive young woman. Mary Alden Hopkins
describes what she looked like:

> *There was something of the china shepherdess in her appearance;*
> *an innocent naughtiness lit up her countenance, quiet fun twinkled*
> *in her large dark eyes and a slight quirk twisted the corners*
> *of her mouth. In figure she was on the small side with just*
> *the right amount of plumpness. She dressed with marked simplicity,*
> *although sometimes in bright colours. Once she went to a party in a*
> *scarlet dress to find the other guests in court mourning and when she*
> *was a very, very old lady she wore a lovely pale green silk*
> *frock with an exquisite Chinese shawl. The embroidered linen caps*
> *which she wore in her old age were dainty and most becoming.*[1]

Charlotte Yonge says she 'was evidently a very pretty girl, with
delicate refined features, rather sharply cut, and beautiful keen
dark eyes, which were enhanced in brilliance by the whiteness
of her powdered hair'.[2] This is borne out by Frances Reynolds's
painting in 1780 of Hannah posing as a writer with quill in hand.
It shows a striking young woman with long dark hair made into

a plait, bright questioning eyes, a sensitive nose and mouth, and long delicate fingers. Opie's later painting in 1787 showing her with a mass of powdered hair was said by Richard Polewhele to have 'hit her likeness, but had lost all the fine expression of her countenance'.[3]

All her life Hannah suffered from ill health, especially from recurring headaches which would sometimes prevent her from writing or studying for days on end. She learned to live with these headaches, making sure that she used her good days to be really productive. But even when she was ill her bright character still managed to shine through. On one occasion, when still a teenager, she was really quite unwell and her doctor, Dr Woodward, came to see her. The conversation turned to literature and Hannah so enthralled the doctor with the subject that he quite forgot the purpose of his visit. Half-way down the stairs the doctor cried out, 'Bless me! I forgot to ask the girl how she was'; and, returning to the room, he exclaimed, 'How are you today, my poor child?'[4]

Hannah More was not lacking in suitors. The first to offer her his hand was a middle-aged squire, almost twenty years her senior, Edward Turner of Belmont, Wraxall. (Wraxall is a small village to the south of Bristol.) Turner's two female cousins attended the Park Street school and were accustomed to spend their holidays at Belmont. Turner had a large house, carriages and horses. The girls were encouraged to bring friends to stay with them and, as the younger More girls were nearly the same age, invited Hannah and Patty to stay. Turner became attached to Hannah, they enjoyed romantic walks in the woods round Belmont, and Hannah wrote verses which Turner fixed to trees around the estate. When Turner proposed marriage, it must have been a tempting offer to a young and impoverished schoolteacher. Hannah accepted, gave up her post in the school, and purchased her trousseau at some considerable expense.

According to Thomas de Quincey, a not wholly impartial reporter, the bridegroom three times postponed the wedding day, and on the third occasion jilted Hannah at the church. While the bride and her friends awaited him in Clifton Church, the bridegroom excused himself with a note of apology brought by the best man. It was, says the perceptive Charlotte Yonge, the case of 'an elderly man growing shy'. Hannah was in any event prevailed upon to break the engagement which had lasted for some six years. Her friends took matters in hand, and Dr Stonehouse,

24

without Hannah's knowledge or consent, reached an agreement with Turner for settling an annuity upon her. This was for £200 a year, a sum less than that offered by Turner, but enough to give her financial independence.

Turner always spoke of Hannah with the greatest respect. His first glass of wine every day, whether alone or in company, was a solemn toast to Hannah. Her inscriptions remained affixed to the trees of Belmont and a cottage in the grounds was named after her. Several of Hannah's poems were inspired by Belmont. A rust-streaked rock in the grounds was behind her *Ballad of Bleeding Rock*, subtitled *The Metamorphosis of a Nymph into Stone*, which was based on a poem by Ovid and told the tale of a nymph's desertion by her faithless lover. Turner, the faithless lover, seems to have borne Hannah no grudge for the poem. For her part Hannah showed no signs of carrying any lasting ill will against her bashful squire. Some twenty years later Turner met Hannah again when riding past her cottage at Cowslip Green. Their friendship was renewed and Turner became an occasional visitor. On his death he bequeathed Hannah £1,000.

Hannah was twenty-eight years of age at the time of the breaking of her engagement to Turner. She had lost the prospect of a secure and comfortable marriage and she must have felt cheated and forsaken. Her health was never good at the best of times and she suffered what was quaintly called 'a morbid sensibility of constitution', but which was in all probability a reactive depressive illness. To recover she went down to stay at Weston-super-Mare. There she met Dr John Langhorne, the Somerset poet and translator of the Greek biographer Plutarch. Langhorne, who had married for the second time a few years before meeting Hannah, was himself recovering from illness. The two convalescents rode together along the beach and left verses for each other in a cleft post. Once Langhorne wrote in the sand with his cane:

Along the shore walked Hannah More,
Waves! Let this record last;
Sooner shall ye proud earth and sea,
Than what she writes, be past.

Hannah replied in similar fashion by writing with her riding whip:

Some firmer base, polished Langhorne, choose,
To write the dictates of your charming muse,

Thy strains in solid characters rehearse,
And be thy tablet lasting as thy verse.

So began a platonic and literary friendship between these two budding poets. Langhorne was an excellent letter writer and often chided Hannah in strongly ironic tones for not seeing him more often. Hannah obviously thought enough of Langhorne to retain his letters until her death.

Blagdon House, 12th Feb. 1775

My Dear Madam,

When I found that you had slipped away to London, without any more regard to your promise than a prime minister, I opened your letter in no good temper, you may suppose. But I had not read far than I began to soften, by and by to be appeased, then satisfied, and afterwards in perfect good humour; and all this for no reason in the world, that I could discover, but because some folks have a knack in writing, and like Milton's very polite and sensible devil, can make 'the worse appear the better reason'.

The lachet *of being thus overcome, however, is perfectly ridiculous; and, now that I have recovered my senses a little, I can see your fault in spite of your address; or, to speak, like my old acquaintance, Dr. I — , 'I can perceive the turpitude of your guilt through the magnetism of your eloquence.'*

In plain English, you were very lazy and very naughty, in not stepping over to Blagdon as you promised. You know my carriage was at your summons. But you do not care a farthing for us, and you are disappointed if you think thereby to make us unhappy; for there is no reason why we should despise ourselves, though you despise us . . .

You are a classic — Vive, memor mei!

J. Langhorne

P.S. — You are so obliging as to ask for commands; supposing that if a poet and a philosopher have business in town, it must doubtless be in your own literary way. Pray be so good as go to the warehouse in George's Yard, Oxford Street, over against Dean Street, Soho, and buy me a bushel of Surinam potatoes for planting; which with the paper of instructions you will receive along with them, please to send by the Bristol waggon, to the Queen's Head, Redcliffe Street.

> *Commands from my lady wife, who is neither poet nor*
> *philosopher, for you or for your good sister, viz. a crimson hat and*
> *cloak trimmed with blond lace. You are moreover desired*
> *to order the necessary materials without leaving a plenipotentiary*
> *commission with the milliner. Neither is to be violently modish. So*
> *saith my lady wife to you and sister, and that she is your*
> *very affectionate humble servant.*[5]

On another occasion Hannah did accept Langhorne's invitation
to visit Blagdon in his carriage. Hannah and Sally one Sunday
morning in May left smoky Bristol for the 'verdure and freshness
of Blagdon'. They stopped at the Bell Inn to freshen up and eat
a breakfast of toast and tea. Arriving at Blagdon they heard Dr
Langhorne preach and went on to the vicarage for dinner with
him and his wife where 'they relished the wine and applauded the
mutton'.[6]

In another letter Langhorne gives us an interesting insight into
the leisured existence of many country parsons of the period. It
shows the intimate but wholly natural relationship between the two
that he should go into such detail:

> *At eight I rise, and that is almost as soon as the sun at this*
> *season makes himself known to us here. On my table I find a cup*
> *of cold chamomile tea with an infusion of orange peel; — dress,*
> *and come down stairs at nine, when I meet my breakfast, consisting*
> *of a basin of lean broth with a dry brown loaf, manufactured from*
> *corn of my own growing. Breakfast table cleared, I call for pen,*
> *ink, and paper, and recollect — not which of my correspondents*
> *I have been longest indebted to, but which the humour leads*
> *most to write to. After this is performed, I apply a little to the laws*
> *of my country, to make myself a more useful citizen, and a*
> *better magistrate. About twelve, if the day turns out fine, I order*
> *my horses, for exercise on Mendip, which at this time of the year*
> *I can seldom effect; I am consequently obliged to seek to exercise in*
> *measuring the length of my own hall. At two I dine, always upon*
> *one dish, and by way of dessert, eat three or four golden pippins,*
> *the produce of my own orchard, and drink as many glasses of wine.*
> *But then the afternoon — the solitary afternoon — Oh! for that*
> *the trash of the month comes in, and whether it makes me laugh or*
> *sleep, 'tis equally useful. The evening is divided between better*
> *books; music, and mending the fire, a roasted potatoe (sic), a pint*
> *basin of punch, and to bed.*

*You have here the whole etiquette of my retirement, which in
the summer is diversified by rural occupations and more agreeable
amusements. In winter I am a better scholar, but in summer
I am a better citizen. In the former season I attend only (as I do in
this letter) to myself; in the latter I cultivate the ground, raise crops
of corn, and hay, and flocks of sheep, and am useful to society.*[7]

Langhorne seems to have been a delightful but rather idle man.
He suffered the misfortune of losing his second wife, who died
in childbirth, and Langhorne himself followed soon afterwards
from grief and excessive drinking. Hannah meantime appears
to have put all thought of marriage behind her, although the
eccentric Scottish peer Lord Monboddo was later unsuccessfully to
propose to her. Hannah enjoyed good and close relationships with
numerous other men: Johnson, Walpole, Newton, Wilberforce and
others. None, however, occupied the place of David Garrick, with
whom there can be little doubt she was quite enamoured, although
their friendship was always highly respectable.

When she came some years later to advise young ladies on the
dangers of what Hannah called 'Sentimental Connections', she
warned them to be on the look-out for 'a dangerous and designing
man, who, by putting on this mask of plausibility and virtue,
disarms (the girl) of her prudence, lays her apprehensions asleep,
and involves her in misery'.[8] The seducer traps the credulous girl
with every kind of adulation and praise and pretends to be totally
uninterested in her marriage dowry. But as soon as the marriage is
complete the hapless bride finds herself discarded.

*She feels herself degraded from the dignities and privileges of
a goddess, to all the imperfections, vanities, and weaknesses of a
slighted woman, and a neglected wife. Her faults, which were
so lately overlooked, or mistaken for virtues, are now, as Cassius
says, set in a note-book. The passion, which was vowed eternal,
lasted only for a few short weeks; and the indifference, which was
so far from being included in the bargain, that it was not so
much as suspected, follows them through the whole tiresome journey
of their insipid, vacant, joyless existence.*[9]

If Hannah was not writing from personal experience of this kind
of seduction, she must have seen enough of unhappy marriages
to write with feeling on the subject. None of the sisters married,
and when Selina Mills, who eventually took over the management

28

of the Park Street school from them, became attached to Zachary Macaulay, they all advised against marriage on the grounds that being married was limiting. The spinster sisters had come to value their singleness as giving them the liberty to pursue interests which might well have been denied them had they been taken up with the consuming matters of marriage and motherhood. Instead of fading into obscurity as the mistress of Belmont, Hannah was now to use her marital freedom and financial independence to launch herself into an altogether more splendid circle of acquaintances.

4

THE LONDON CELEBRITY

I felt myself a worm, the more a worm
for the consequence which was given me,
by mixing me with such a society.

Roberts, *Memoirs*

It was with a great sense of expectation that the young provincial schoolteacher set out to visit London, the scene of many of her day-dreams. She hoped that she might catch sight of Dr Johnson from some hiding-place, and she especially wanted to see the great actor David Garrick before he retired. She tells us that many times she had created for herself an imaginary Thames. When she saw the 'noble current',[1] it was strikingly beautiful as it was all frozen over. It was the winter of 1773-74, when Hannah More, now aged twenty-eight or twenty-nine years, accompanied by two sisters, Sally and Patty, paid her first visit to the capital. An annual visit to London became a feature of Hannah's life for over twenty years, although she never had a house in the capital, and the greater part of each year was spent at the Park Street school and later at her cottage in Somerset. Smart London dinner parties alternated with picnics on the rocks of Bristol's Avon Gorge.

The More sisters stayed in lodgings in Henrietta Street. They spent their first days in London seeing the sights. Hannah was particularly impressed with the British Museum and Hampton Court Palace. She described the latter as more like a town than a palace and so big that she was fearful of getting lost. Like many a tourist Hannah felt the need to take home some mementos of her visits. At the house where Pope had lived, she quite brazenly stole two bits of stone from the grotto, a sprig of laurel from the garden and a pen from one of the bedrooms. Those were the days of collecting not conservation! The sisters also visited Garrick's house at Hampton apparently without seeing the owners. Hannah dismissed it as under repair and not worth visiting. But she did take the opportunity to sit in the famous chair made out of a cherry tree which actually grew in Shakespeare's garden in Stratford. Despite its famous associations and its position in a garden temple overlooking the Thames, Hannah drew no inspiration from it. But she was highly taken with a statue of the Bard, which she records as costing £500, a princely sum for those days.

With the help of Jacob More's old patron, Norborne Berkeley, Hannah was introduced to Mrs Boscawen, widow of Admiral Boscawen. Berkeley was the uncle of the fifth Duke of Beaufort. The Duchess called on Hannah shortly after her arrival in London and introduced Hannah to her mother, Mrs Boscawen. Berkeley also introduced Hannah to Sir Joshua Reynolds, the portrait painter and first President of the Royal Academy. Hannah described Sir Joshua as 'the idol of every company',[2] and at his house she fulfilled her long-felt ambition to meet Dr Samuel Johnson. Sir Joshua had warned Hannah that the great Doctor might be in one of his moods. But Hannah was delighted to find Dr Johnson in jovial spirits, holding a macaw of Sir Joshua's in his hand. He immediately greeted Hannah with a verse from her own poem, *Morning Hymn*. This was a poem about not getting up in the morning written for Dr Stonehouse, who called her a slug-a-bed.

Soft slumbers now my eyes forsake,
My powers are all renew'd;
May my freed spirit too awake,
With heavenly strength endu'd!

Thou silent murderer, SLOTH, no more
My mind imprison'd keep.
Nor let me waste another hour
With thee, thou felon SLEEP.

The Doctor invited the sisters to visit him at his home, 7 Johnson Court. They were accompanied by Sir Joshua's sister, and travelled in the Reynolds' coach attended by silver-liveried footmen. The sisters were overjoyed at the prospect of meeting 'Dictionary Johnson'. 'Can you imagine the palpitation of our hearts as we approached his mansion?' wrote Sally. At Dr Johnson's they met

Mrs Williams, the blind poet and a member of the household, and talked about Johnson's trip to the Hebrides and his book on the journey. Miss Reynolds told Dr Johnson about the sisters' excitement at all they had seen on the road. Dr Johnson 'shook his scientific head at Hannah, and said, "She was a *silly thing*."'[3] In Dr Johnson's little parlour, Hannah seated herself in his great chair, hoping 'to catch a little ray of his genius'. The Doctor laughingly told her that he never sat in that chair. He was very gallant to the ladies and saw them off in the rain. Dr Johnson later told Miss Reynolds how much he had been impressed by the enthusiasm of the young writer, which must have been in marked contrast to the affectations of many in fashionable society. Hannah was that rare person who, in her own words, 'thought it a less evil to dissent from the opinion of a fellow-creature, than to tell a falsity'.[4]

After six weeks in London Hannah went back to Bristol with her sisters but returned the following February. She wrote home:

London 1775

> *Our first visit was to Sir Joshua's, where we were received with all the friendship imaginable. I am going, today, to a great dinner; nothing can be conceived so absurd, extravagant and fantastical, as the present mode of dressing the head. Simplicity and modesty are things so much exploded, that the very names are no longer remembered. I have just escaped from one of the most fashionable disfigurers; and though I charged him to dress me with the greatest simplicity, and to have only a very distant eye upon the fashion, just enough to avoid the pride of particularity, without running into ridiculous excess; yet in spite of these sage didactics, I absolutely blush at myself, and turn to the glass with as much caution as a vain beauty, just risen from the small-pox; which cannot be a more disfiguring disease than the present mode of dressing.[5]*

Hannah was a keen observer of fashion and customs and did not like much of what she saw. She wrote to her sister, 'And now that we are upon vanities, what do you think is the reigning mode as to powder? — only tumerick, that coarse dye that stains yellow . . . It falls out of the hair and stains the skin so, that every pretty lady must look as yellow as a crocus.'[6] She deplored haughty ladies who wore elaborate hats, but looked down on useful members of society who carried things on their head for a living. Such extravagances were not limited to London society ladies; when Hannah visited her cousins in East Anglia, she observed wryly that the ladies present in one gathering carried an acre and a half of shrubbery on their heads, and flowers as well. Nor was she impressed by the behaviour of the nobility. She saw it as a signal from heaven when a sumptuously dressed relation of the Duchess of Chandos dropped dead when playing cards. And Hannah was horrified to hear that when an upper-class hotel was opened in St James Street, some sixty thousand pounds was lost on the card table in one night.

Hannah now began to move freely in a select literary circle, which centred around David Garrick, Dr Johnson and Sir Joshua Reynolds. It also included a number of literary ladies, particularly Mrs Montagu, Mrs Carter and Mrs Boscawen. Reynolds and his sister, Frances, in their home in Leicester Square were particularly hospitable; and they became the social honey-pot around which the others were happy to swarm. Hannah relished the intellectual stimulus of such a cultured society. Although she felt herself inadequate, she was more than able to hold her own. She was after all fluent in French and conversant in Italian, Spanish and Latin, and was well read in all these languages, as she was in English.

Dr Johnson, although nearly forty years older than Hannah seems to have taken quite a fancy to the young woman. She was not overawed by the great man's reputation. Together they read Hannah's poems and Dr Johnson commended Hannah to James Beattie as 'the most powerful versificatrix in the English language'. Sally reported home:

> *Tuesday evening we drank tea at Sir Joshua's, with Dr Johnson.*
> *Hannah is certainly a great favourite. She was placed next to*
> *him, and they had the entire conversation to themselves. They were*
> *both in remarkably high spirits; it was certainly her lucky night!*
> *I never heard her say so many good things. The old genius*
> *was extremely jocular, and the young one very pleasant. You*
> *would have imagined we had been at some comedy had you heard*
> *our peals of laughter. They, indeed, tried which could 'pepper the*
> *highest', and it is not clear to me that the lexicographer was really*
> *the highest seasoner.*[7]

Later, when Hannah escorted the Doctor home, Mrs Montagu asked whether she could trust the two of them together as she was afraid of a Scottish elopement. It was, of course, said in jest, but the friendship between the two was obvious to their friends. The young provincial woman seemed to bring a touch of fresh air to the stuffy atmosphere of London life. On one occasion Johnson came to tea and stayed until midnight. They were so taken up in their conversation and the reading of *Sir Eldred* and *The Rock* that they never bothered to eat a thing, and only drank tea. Hannah told her sisters that they would have fidgeted to death and 'sent half over the town for chickens, and oysters, and asparagus, and Madeira'.[8] In a letter the romantically minded Sally told her Bristol sisters:

> *If a wedding should take place upon our return, don't be surprised, — between the mother of Sir Eldred [Hannah], and the father of my much-loved Irene [Dr Johnson]; nay, Mrs Montagu says if tender words are the precursors of connubial engagements, we may expect great things; for it is nothing but 'child' — 'little fool' — 'love', and 'dearest'.[9]*

When Dr Johnson asked Sally how the sisters got themselves into 'the useful and honourable employment of teaching young ladies', and Sally told him, the Doctor responded with zest:

> *'I love you both', cried the inamorato — 'I love you all five — I never was at Bristol — but I will come on purpose to see you — what! five women living happily together! — I will come and see you — I have spent a happy evening — I am glad I came — God forever bless you, you live lives to shame duchesses.' He took his leave with so much warmth and tenderness, we were quite affected at his manner.[10]*

The Doctor kept his word and visited what he delighted to call the Sisterhood in Bristol on 29 April 1776. He came over from Bath to Bristol as part of his investigations into the boy poet, Thomas Chatterton, who had died so unhappily six years earlier. Some time later Hannah met up with Dr Johnson at a dinner at the residence of the Bishop of Chester, Dr Porteus. The couple sat side by side, the Doctor holding Hannah's hand, repeating passages from her poetry and telling her that she should have married her fellow townsman, Chatterton, so 'that posterity might have a propagation of poets'. Urged by Hannah to take a little wine, Dr Johnson replied, 'I can't drink a little, child, therefore I never touch it. Abstinence is as easy to me as temperance would be difficult.'[11]

The Doctor liked to tease Hannah about her religious views. She even managed to persuade him that there were some good men, and even some good writers, among the Puritans. After a day spent with Dr Johnson and Mrs Williams at the Reynolds', Hannah wrote home:

We did not part till eleven. He scolded me heartily as usual,
when I differed from him in opinion, and, as usual, laughed when
I flattered him . . . I never saw Johnson really angry with me
but once, and his displeasure did him so much honour that I loved
him the better for it. I alluded rather flippantly, I fear, to some
witty passages in Tom Jones. *He replied: 'I am shocked to*
hear you have read it; a confession which no modest lady should
make. I scarcely know a more corrupt work.' I thanked him
for his correction.[12]

Some years later, in 1782, Johnson, then aged seventy-three, showed obvious pleasure in escorting Hannah around Oxford. In the common room of his old college, Pembroke, they came across a large print of the Doctor himself, inscribed with a line from Hannah's own poem, *Sensibility* 'And is not Johnson in himself a host?'

That Hannah More is not better known can in part be attributed to Boswell. He formed a hearty dislike of the woman who dared to criticize him for his drinking. Boswell pointedly omitted all reference to her in his biography of Johnson. Hannah's flirtation with Johnson was never more than a playful and mutual admiration. It was the actor-manager David Garrick who occupied first place in Hannah's sentiments and who inspired her most creative writing.

When Hannah first went up to London she carried an introduction from Dr Stonehouse to Garrick and his Austrian wife, Eva Maria. Garrick had apparently been flattered by Hannah's enthusiastic description, in a letter to a mutual friend, of his performance as Lear. But Garrick was ill when Hannah arrived in London. She reported to her friend Mrs Gwatkin:

He is not well enough to play or see company — how mortifying!
He has been at Hampton for a week. If he does not get well
enough to act soon, I shall break my heart.[13]

David Garrick was famous as an actor, producer and dramatist. He was thought to have brought a revolutionary new style of natural interpretative acting to the English stage. He became co-manager of the Drury Lane Theatre in 1747, and retired from the theatre in 1776. David Garrick's wife, Eva Maria, was a dancer from Vienna who went under the stage name of La Violette. Rumour had it that the Empress Maria Theresa was so disturbed by the Emperor's admiration for the lovely young girl, that she had her sent to

London to be put in the care of Lady Burlington. In London Eva met and married David Garrick. The Garricks formed an extremely engaging and hospitable couple. David Garrick was one of the first actors to be accepted in London high society at a time when actors tended to be looked down on by upper-class people, and were regarded as pursuing a somewhat dubious profession.

When they met Hannah the Garricks were entranced by the learning and charm of the young visitor. They nicknamed her Nine as the personification of the nine Muses. A lifelong friendship blossomed on both sides and the Garrick homes were ever open to receive Hannah. Hannah rejoiced to find a household where the conversation was intellectual rather than mere social gossip and tittle-tattle, where cards were not played, and where there was a happy mixture of humour and propriety. Hannah wrote from Hampton:

> *We have been passing three days at the temple of taste, nature, Shakespeare and Garrick; where every thing that could please the ear, charm the eye, and gratify the understanding, passed in quick succession. From dinner to midnight he entertained us in a manner infinitely agreeable. He read to us all the whimsical correspondence, in prose and verse, which, for many years, he had carried on with the first geniuses of this age. I have now seen him in his mellower light, when the world has been shaken off.[14]*

And later:

> *I am so much at my ease; have a great many hours at my own disposal, to read my books and see my friends; and, whenever I please, may join the most polished and delightful society in the world! Our breakfasts are little literary societies; there is generally company at meals, as they think it saves time, by avoiding the necessity of seeing people at other seasons . . . From dinner to tea we laugh, chat and talk nonsense . . . I detest and avoid public places more than ever, and should make a miserably bad fine lady. What most people come to London for, would keep me from it.[15]*

The Garricks had a house in the Adelphi, London, which was in the most exquisite taste. The house was built by Robert Adam and furnished by Chippendale, the leading furniture-maker of the day. It had a handsome dining-room with a carved marble fireplace and a lovely ceiling painted by Angelica Kauffmann, which is preserved in the Victoria and Albert Museum. Garrick loved to entertain at the Adelphi, especially to late breakfasts which suited his way of life as an actor. The Garricks also maintained a house at Hampton, then a semi-rural suburb of London. Their house was separated by a road from the garden, which sloped down to the Thames. Garrick built an underpass to reach the garden. It was in this garden that the eccentric Scottish peer, Lord Monboddo, proposed marriage to Hannah. She turned down his offer. Later Lord Monboddo said, 'I am very sorry for this refusal. I should so much have liked to have taught this nice girl Greek.' After Garrick's death he also proposed marriage to Eva Maria. Her garden, he said, was perfect. It was a paradise lacking only Adam![16]

During 1777 Hannah visited Farnsworth Place, the home of the Henry Wilmots. There, among the other guests, she formed friendships which were to continue through to the third generation. The Lord Chancellor, Lord Bathurst, and his wife lived in great style at Apsley House at Hyde Park Corner. In later years Lady Bathurst and 'her fair train' of four spinster daughters used to call on the Mores at Barley Wood. Also at the house party were Dr Kennicott, a famous Hebrew scholar, and his wife, who had learned Hebrew so as to read to him. It was at Farnsworth that Garrick sensitively came to Hannah's rescue when her sabbatarian principles were offended by her host's proposal to play music, albeit sacred music, on a Sunday evening. Garrick turned to Hannah and said in his familiar way, 'Nine, you are a Sunday *woman*; retire to your room — I will recall you when the music is over.'[17]

Years later when Hannah wrote the following lines about the value of Sunday as a time to recharge the spiritual batteries she was undoubtedly setting the pattern for the celebrated Victorian sabbath:

To the Christian in the world . . . the Sunday is felt to be indeed a blessing; to him it is emphatically 'a delight' . . . He considers the observance as almost more his privilege than his duty. The expectation of its return cheers him under the perplexities of the week . . . It is an appointment of God; that entitles it to his reverence; it is an institution of spiritual mercy; it is the stated season for recruiting his mental vigour; for inspecting his accounts with his Maker; for taking a more exact survey of the state of his heart; for examining into his faults; for enumerating his mercies; for laying in, by prayer, fresh stores of faith and holiness; for repairing what may have been lost in the turmoil of the

week. His heated passions have leisure to cool; his hurried mind to
regain its tranquil tone; his whole internal state to be regulated; his
mistakes to be reviewed; his temper to be new set; his piety
to be braced up to the pitch from which it may have been sunk in
the atmosphere he had been breathing. The pious man of business
relishes his family society and fire-side enjoyments with a keenness
not always felt by others.[18]

Already the tension was beginning to emerge between Hannah's
growing religious convictions and the fashion of that world in which
she was such a bright new luminary. Hannah was fortunate with
her new London friends. She admired Sir Joshua Reynolds for not
being 'ashamed to take his subjects from the most unfashionable
of books',[19] the Bible, about which upper-class society seems to
have been woefully ignorant. (Sir Joshua, once when showing his
painting of Samuel to some of the great, was astonished to be asked
who Samuel was.) Also, Dr Stonehouse kept an eye on his young
protégée from afar. As early as 1775 Hannah was writing home:

Thank my dear Dr S — for his kind and seasonable admonitions
on my last Sunday's engagement at Mrs Montagu's. Conscience
had done its office before; nay, was busy at the time: and if it did
not dash the cup of pleasure to the ground, infused at least
a tincture of wormwood into it. I did think of the alarming call,
'What doest thou here, Elijah?' and I thought of it to-night
at the opera.[20]

5
THE BLUE STOCKING

The women of this country were not sent
into this world to shun society,
but to embellish it.

Essays

'All the world of dukes, lords and barons were there. I sat next to a baron and a lord. All expressed the highest approbation of the whole.'[1] So wrote an enthusiastic Sally about Hannah's first tragic play, *The Inflexible Captive*, after the play's première at the Theatre Royal, Bath, in April 1775. *The Inflexible Captive* was a story of patriotism, honour and virtue. Based on Hannah's own translation of the lyrical drama by the Italian writer, Metastasio, it told the story of the Roman hero, Marcus Attilius Regulus, a prisoner of war, who was returned to Rome by the Carthaginians to negotiate peace. Regulus honourably advised against the peace terms forced upon him and returned to Carthage in accordance with the terms of his oath to suffer inevitable death.

The prologue was written by Hannah's old literary friend, the Reverend Dr John Langhorne. The epilogue by Garrick defended Hannah against male prejudice in the form of a drunken fop who argued:

A woman write? Learn, madam, of your betters,
And read a noble lord's posthumous letters.
There you may learn the sex may merit praise
By making puddings — not by making plays;
They can make tea and mischief, dance and sing;
Their heads, though full of feathers, can't take wing.

The lord referred to in the poem was the Earl of Chesterfield

Garrick's response was to cite Milton in defence of the fairest and best of God's creation, and to point to the achievements of Mrs Montagu in defending Shakespeare against Voltaire, of Mrs Carter, who 'can boast ten tongues', and of Hannah herself. All these women were to become members of a largely female literary circle known as the Blue Stockings. According to Fanny Burney, one of their number, the Blue Stockings took their name not from the colour of the ladies' hosiery, which was of course discreetly covered, but from that of the stockings worn by Dr Benjamin Stillingfleet. On one occasion when invited to a gathering of the ladies, Stillingfleet found himself with no appropriate dress, but came at the insistence of Mrs Vesey in his workaday blue ribbed stockings.

Hannah was introduced to 'the petticoteries', as Horace Walpole liked to call them, by Mrs Elizabeth Montagu. Mrs Montagu, 'The Queen of the Bees', was a scanty writer but a woman of wealth, generosity and intellect. She organized these 'conversation' evenings in an attempt to find a more worthy pastime than playing cards. She entertained splendidly in her London home, later a magnificent mansion in Portman Square, and also in her country house, Saddleford Priory, near Newbury. The Blue Stockings, who were never in any sense a formal society, were made up of affluent hostesses like Mrs Montagu, Mrs Thrale and Mrs Vesey; intellectual women like the learned Mrs Carter, the plain-featured Mrs Chapone, the beautiful Mrs Crewe, the shy novelist and letter writer Fanny Burney and the eccentric Miss Mary Monckton; and ladies of rank and fortune like Lady Mary Bute, Mrs Boscawen and her two daughters, the Duchess of Beaufort and Mrs Leveson. Distinguished men of letters such as Horace Walpole, Samuel Johnson, Sir Joshua Reynolds and Lord Lyttleton were honoured guests at these conversation parties.

In a short time Hannah More became the acknowledged poet of the Blues. Her fame had reached its literary zenith, eclipsing even that of the scholarly schoolmistress, Mrs Carter, the translator of Epictetus. She received this accolade from Mrs Thrale, 'I think Hannah More is the cleverest of all us female wits.'[2] Certainly Hannah is included in the *Ladies Pocket Book of 1778* among the Nine Muses along with Mrs Carter, Angelica Kauffmann, Elizabeth Montagu and others. In her poem *Bas Bleu*, Hannah described how the prevailing pursuits of the leisured classes were replaced in this elite circle:

> Long was society o'er-run
> By whist, that desolating Hun;
> Long did quadrille despotic sit,
> That Vandal of colloquial wit;
> And conversation's setting light
> Lay half-obscur'd in Gothic night;
>
> At length the mental shades decline,
> Colloquial wit begins to shine;
> Genius prevails, and conversation
> Emerges into reformation.
>
> Here chaste duchesses are seen,
> Chaste wits and critics void of spleen;
> Physicians, fraught with real science,
> And Whigs and Tories in alliance.
>
> Learn'd antiquaries, who, from college,
> Reject the dust, and bring the knowledge;
> And hear it, age, believe it, youth, —
> Polemics really seeking truth;
> And travellers of that rare tribe,
> Who've seen the countries they describe.

Hannah's poem *Sir Eldred and the Bower* shows her interest in the then current revival of English legends. Sir Eldred, a gallant knight, loves Birtha, but finds her embracing a strange knight in the garden. Sir Eldred promptly kills the intruder. Unfortunately Birtha had forgotten to tell her lover that she had a long-missing brother, and it is this brother whom Sir Eldred has killed. His jealousy leads to despair, madness and death. Her *Ballad of the Bleeding Rock* revives memories of Edward Turner of Belmont, 'where beauteous Belmont rears her modest brow to view Sabrina's (the River Severn) silver wave below'. But in truth Hannah had left Turner far behind in mind and sentiment.

Hannah found that she was not happy in the enormous assemblies in which London society rejoiced. Sensible conversation was impossible in the great crush of humanity, and people attended for nothing more than to see and be seen. She preferred more intimate gatherings with her friends. This suited Dr Johnson as well, since he

43

was rather deaf and could hear next to nothing in a crowded room. In one letter to her family, Hannah described a dinner party that she and Sally gave in their lodgings for seven guests: Dr Johnson, Frances Reynolds, Mrs Boscawen, the Reverend Josiah Tucker, the Dean of Gloucester, and the Garricks. Hannah wrote:

> *Garrick was the very soul of the party and I never saw Johnson in such perfect good humour. Sally knows that one has often heard that one can never enjoy the company of these two unless they are together. There is great truth in this remark; for after the Dean and Mrs Boscawen (who were the only strangers) were withdrawn, and the rest stood up to go, Johnson and Garrick began a close encounter telling old stories e'en from their boyish days in Lichfield. We all stood around them about an hour, laughing and in defiance of every rule of decorum and Chesterfield. I believe that we would not have thought of sitting down or parting, had not an impertinent watchman been saucily vociferous. Johnson outstayed them all and sat with me an half an hour.*
>
>   *I'll tell you the most ridiculous circumstance in the world. After dinner, Garrick took up the Monthly Review (civil gentlemen, by-the-by, these Monthly Reviewers) and read Sir Eldred with all his pathos and all his graces. I think I was never so ashamed in all my life; but he read it so superlatively that I cried like a child. Only think what a scandalous thing to do, to cry at the reading of one's own poetry! I could have beaten myself: for it looked as if I thought it very moving, which, I can truly say, is far from being the case. But the jest lies in this: Mrs. Garrick twinkled as well as I, and made as many apologies at crying at her husband's reading, as I did for crying at my own verses. She got out of the scrape by pretending that she was touched at the story, and I by saying the same thing for the reading. It furnished me with a great laugh at the catastrophe, when it would really have been decent to have been a little sorrowful!*[3]

Garrick retired from the stage in 1776. Hannah confessed to having seen Garrick act twenty-seven times in one season. She was ecstatic about all his performances, especially those as Hamlet and King Lear. In a letter to Mrs Gwatkin she described him as 'one of those summer suns, which shine brightest at their setting'.[4] Hannah wrote to Garrick himself on 10 June 1776 at the time of the American War of Independence:

44

I have devoured the newspapers for the last week with the appetite
of a famished politician, to learn if my general had yet laid down
arms; but I find you go on with a true American spirit, destroying
thousands of his Majesty's liege subjects, destroying the limbs
of many, and the hearts of all . . . I think, by the time this reaches
you, I may congratulate you on the end of your labours and
the completion of your fame — a fame which has no parallel, and
will have no end. Yet whatever reputation the world may ascribe
to you, I, who have had the happy privilege of knowing you
intimately, shall always think you derived the greatest glory from
the temperance with which you enjoyed it, and the true greatness of
mind with which you laid it down.[5]

To mark Garrick's retirement from the stage, Hannah wrote an
Ode to Dragon, Mr. Garrick's Housedog at Hampton.

Peace ! — To his solitude he bears
The full-blown fame of thirty years;
He bears a nation's praise;
He bears his lib'ral, polish'd mind,
His worth, his wit, his sense refin'd;
He bears his well-earn'd bays.

When warm admirers drop a tear,
Because this sun has left his sphere,
And set before his time;
I who have felt and lov'd his rays,
What they condemn will loudly praise,
And call the deed sublime.

How wise! long pamper'd with applause,
To make a voluntary pause
And lay his laurels down!
Boldly repelling each strong claim,
To dare assert to wealth and fame,
'Enough of both I've known.'
How wise! a short retreat to steal,
The vanity of life to feel,
And from its cares to fly;
To act one calm, domestic scene,
Earth's bustle and the grave between,
Retire, and learn to die!

In May 1777 Hannah brought out *Essays on Various Subjects Principally Designed for Young Ladies*. The book was dedicated to Mrs Montagu. Hannah offered her views on the differences between the sexes:

> *Besides those important qualities common to both, each sex*
> *has its respective, appropriate qualities, which would cease to be*
> *meritorious, the instant they ceased to be appropriated. Nature,*
> *propriety and custom have prescribed certain bounds to each;*
> *bounds which the prudent and the candid will never attempt*
> *to break down; as indeed it would be highly impolitic to annihilate*
> *distinctions from which each acquires excellence, and to attempt*
> *innovations by which both would be losers.*[6]

Hannah, like many of her generation, believed that women 'find their protection in their weakness, and their safety in their delicacy'. By contrast, men 'are formed for the more public exhibitions on the great theatre of human life . . . They were intended by Providence for the bustling scenes of life; to appear terrible in arms, useful in commerce, shining in counsels.'[7] Women are fine porcelain; men are rough earthenware. She thought the female mind not as capable as the male in matters of science, but possibly superior in matters of taste.

> *Women have generally quicker perceptions; men have juster*
> *sentiments. Women consider how things may be prettily said; men*
> *how they may be properly said. In women (young ones at least)*
> *speaking accompanies, and sometimes precedes reflection; in men,*
> *reflection is the antecedent. Women speak to shine or to please;*
> *men, to convince or confute. Women admire what is brilliant; men,*
> *what is solid . . . Women are fond of incident; men, of*
> *argument. Women admire passionately; men approve cautiously.*
> *One sex will think it betrays a want of feeling to be moderate in*
> *their applause; the other will be afraid of exposing a want*
> *of judgment by being in raptures with any thing. Men refuse to give*
> *way to the emotions they actually feel, while women sometimes*
> *affect to be transported beyond what the occasion will justify.*[8]

If these comments seem alien to modern feminist sentiments, we need to remind ourselves that Hannah was writing for an age which knew nothing of female suffrage, of higher education for girls or of equal job opportunities for the sexes. Hannah was not arguing for female inferiority but for sexual differentiation. She would, we may suppose, have highly approved of the enormous advances in the status of women in this century. She was herself strongly in favour of the mixed society of the sexes, believing that women could refine and polish male behaviour. Far from thinking that women should be seen and not heard, she argued that they should not be afraid to speak their knowledge or learning. And in a society which did not put its women into purdah, she was convinced of the enormous civilizing influence of women.

> *The prevailing manners of an age depend more than we are aware, or are willing to allow, on the conduct of the women: this is one of the principal hinges on which the great machine of human society turns . . . How much it is to be regretted, that the British ladies should ever sit down contented to polish, when they are able to reform; to entertain, when they might instruct; and to dazzle for an hour, when they are candidates for eternity!*[9]

> *The women of this country were not sent into the world to shun society, but to embellish it: they were not designed for wilds and solitudes, but for the amiable and endearing offices of social life. They have useful stations to fill, and important characters to sustain. They are of a religion . . . which does not condemn its followers to indolent seclusion from the world, but assigns them the dangerous though more honourable province, of living uncorrupted by it.*[10]

Hannah's year of 1777 was crowned by the production of her second major play, *Percy*, a tragedy in five acts, at the Theatre Royal, Drury Lane. The play was performed to crowded and enthusiastic audiences in December and ran for twenty-two nights into January. This was considered a long run for those days when other plays had flopped at Drury Lane. The critics were kind and Hannah was flattered to see even the men shed tears in abundance. She confessed, 'I have had so much flattery, that I might, if I would choke myself in my own pap.'[11] *Percy* was a Border drama of the great houses of Douglas and Percy at the time of the Crusades. Mrs Barry played the heroine, Elwina, who is forced by her father to marry Earl Douglas, the enemy of her true love, Percy, Earl of Northumberland. The play ends in total tragedy showing the folly of human jealousy and revenge. The jealous husband, Douglas, kills Percy; Elwina commits suicide with poison, and the contrite Douglas stabs himself to death.

The play probably represents the zenith of Hannah's poetic powers. It contains some fine lines and is notable for its strong sentiments about the error of 'fanatic wars', particularly under the guise of religion. It must be remembered that England was fighting the American War of Independence at the time. Hannah admitted to being nervous about how the anti-war speech would be received, especially when she noted the Prime Minister's wife, Lady North, in the audience. But it seems to have drawn only warm applause:

'Tis not the crosier, nor the pontiff's robe,
Nor outward show, nor form of sanctity,
Nor Palestine destroy'd, nor Jordan's banks
Delug'd with blood of slaughter'd infidels,
No, nor the extinction of the Eastern world,
Nor all the wild, pernicious bigot rage
Of mad crusades, can bribe that Pow'r, who sees
The motive with the act. O, blind to think
Fanatic wars can please the Prince of Peace!
He who erects his altar in the heart,
Abhors the sacrifice of human blood,
And hates the false devotion of that zeal
Which massacres the world he died to save.

The author's royalties were £600, quite a fortune for the day. Her publisher, Cadell, paid £150 for the copyright of the play and confessed that he had made a great deal of money out of its publication. The first edition of four thousand sold out within a fortnight. *Percy* was revived several times until 1815, and played at Drury Lane and the Haymarket as well as Bath and Bristol. It was translated into French and played in German in Vienna. Among the most fulsome admirers was John Heard, who wrote the poem, *Impromptu on Seeing Miss More's Tragedy of Percy*, which ended with the far from immortal lines:

Each auditor with loud applause,
Confessed the fair had won the cause,
And cried MORE? MORE, yes MORE.

Earl Northumberland and his son, Lord Percy, conveyed their thanks for the honour done to them by the play and regretted that gout had kept them away. Lord Lyttleton was said to have attended every night. Hannah told her sister, 'I believe it was a false delicacy, but I could not go to anybody's house, for fear they should think I came to be praised or to hear the play talked of.'[12] During the play's run, Hannah was taken ill. Garrick, who wrote both the prologue and the epilogue, visited her every day and always found her cheerful and patient. On one occasion Garrick brought in his coach a stew pan of minced chicken, a canister of tea and a pot of cream for Hannah's dinner. It is an indication of the happy relationship between the two that one day Garrick announced that he had ordered mourning for himself and that Eva wished to know what inscription Hannah wanted on her grave. Hannah replied that she had delegated this to Dr Johnson, but as she thought Garrick would praise her more, she would be happy to change.[13]

Hannah's third tragic drama was *Fatal Falsehood*. Its story centres around the familiar love triangle. Orlando, although engaged to Emmaline, falls in love with Julia, the betrothed of his friend Rivers. The villain, Bertram, is madly jealous of Rivers, who stands between him and his uncle's inheritance, and seeks to murder him. Orlando accidentally kills Bertram in the garden at night but thinks that he has killed Rivers. Orlando commits suicide and Emmaline dies apparently from madness caused by slighted love, which conveniently leaves the stage clear for Rivers and Julia to finish in each other's arms. The plot is clumsy and contrived, but the production was good and the play had an excellent cast for its performance at the Theatre Royal, Covent Garden. It ran for only four nights, but the famous actress Mrs Siddons was later to play in both *Percy* and *Fatal Falsehood* at Bath. The sequel to the play was an ill-tempered dispute with Mrs Parkhouse Cowley, who accused Hannah of stealing *Fatal Falsehood* from her unpublished play, *Albina*, a charge which Hannah vigorously denied.

In 1778 Hannah attended her last party with David Garrick.

I dined with the Garricks on Thursday. He went with me in the evening, intending only to set me down at Sir Joshua's, where I was engaged to pass the evening. I was not a little proud to be the means of bringing such a bear into such a company. We found Gibbon, Johnson, Hermes Harris, Burney, Chambers, Ramsey, the Bishop of Asaph, Boswell, Langton and so forth, and scarcely an expletive man among them. Garrick put Johnson into such good spirits that I never knew him so entertaining or more instructive. He was as brilliant as himself, and as good humoured as anyone else.[14]

Garrick died on 20 January 1779. Hannah was greatly distressed. On hearing of Garrick's death she, at Eva's request, rushed up to London. Hannah wrote home describing the meeting with Eva Garrick:

> *She ran into my arms, and we both remained silent for some*
> *minutes; at last she whispered, 'I have this moment embraced*
> *his coffin, and you come next.' She soon recovered herself, and said*
> *with great composure, 'The goodness of God to me is inexpressible;*
> *I desired to die, but it is his will that I should live . . . I*
> *can never cease to remember with affection and gratitude, so warm,*
> *steady and disinterested a friend; and I can most truly bear*
> *this testimony to his memory, that I never witnessed, in any family,*
> *more decorum, propriety and regularity than in his.'[15]*

She wrote to Garrick's friend and solicitor, 'Oh Sir! what a friend have I lost! My heart is almost broken! I have never eaten or slept since. My tears blind me as I write . . . '[16] Hannah and the daughter of Garrick's physician, Miss Cadogan, attended the funeral in Westminster Abbey. The funeral procession contained thirty-three mourning coaches which took two hours to reach the Abbey from the Adelphi, a distance of under a mile. The pallbearers were drawn from the highest in the land including the Duke of Devonshire, Lord Camden and Lord Palmerston. Hannah and Miss Cadogan at one point found themselves inadvertently locked in a tower for some half an hour, but after being rescued they were rewarded with a prize view of the service from a little gallery over the south transept in what is now Poets' Corner.

Hannah wrote home:

> *So passes the fashion of the world. And the very night he was*
> *buried, the playhouses were as full, and the Pantheon as crowded,*
> *as if no such thing had happened: nay, the very mourners of the*
> *day partook of the revelries of the night, — the same night too![17]*

Garrick left no small legacies and Hannah was not mentioned in his will. But Garrick had earlier given Hannah the shoe buckles which formed part of his last stage costume, and an inkstand from what was said to be Shakespeare's mulberry tree. If ever Hannah adored a man it was David Garrick. Mary Alden Hopkins, commenting on Hannah's relationship with Garrick, says, 'It pleased her mind, her ambition, her vanity and most of all her heart.'[18]

50

After Garrick's death Hannah stayed on with Eva to keep her company. Hannah describes their very quiet life. After breakfast the two women retired to their rooms to read. At four they dined. At six they had coffee. At eight they had tea with a dowager lady or two of rank. At ten they had salad and fruit before going to bed. Hannah wrote home:

> Her garden and her family amuse her; but the idea of company is death to her. We never see a human face but each other's. Though in such deep retirement, I am never dull because I am not reduced to the fatigue of entertaining dunces, or being obliged to listen to them. We dress like a couple of scaramouches, dispute like a couple of Jesuits, eat like a couple of aldermen, walk like a couple of porters, and read as much as any two doctors of either university.[19]

Despite Hannah's stated preference for solitude, her personality needed the company of others to blossom. Eva Garrick encouraged Hannah to visit on her own. So it was that Hannah spent time with the venerable Mrs Delany now living with the royal family at Hampton Court, and with Mary Hamilton, who invited Hannah to St James' Palace where she was in attendance on the royal princesses. Later with Eva she visited the elderly Duchess of Portland at Bulstrode. Hannah continued this pattern of staying in London for the winter season with Eva Garrick for some twenty years. The two women shared a common bond in their grief for the beloved David, and Eva found not only friendship but also spiritual strength in the young woman whom she delighted to call her domestic chaplain. Eva was a Catholic but sympathetic towards the Church of England and its Book of Common Prayer.

Garrick died before the performance of *Fatal Falsehood*, and Hannah never again wrote for the stage. She had written when he retired:

> Who shall supply his loss to the stage? Who shall now hold the master-key of the human heart? Who direct the passions with more than magic power? Who purify the stage; and who, in short, shall direct and nurse my dramatic muse?[20]

The answer was that without Garrick there was no one to direct Hannah's dramatic muse, and it perished in the grave with her hero. More than that she lost her love for that world in which Garrick had shone so brilliantly. Years later Hannah confessed to a friend that she would have found retirement from the world all the harder had Garrick lived. During Garrick's farewell season Hannah had stated:

> *I find my dislike of what are called public diversions greater than ever, except a play; and when Garrick has left the stage, I could be very well to relinquish plays also, and to live in London, without ever again setting foot in a public place.*[21]

From the beginning of her time in London, Hannah displayed an uneasy conscience. Initially this was reserved for the opera rather than the theatre. The theatre could have an improving purpose but opera was 'a wondrous waste', and written in a language most people did not understand. In 1775 Hannah had written to her sister, 'Going to the opera, like getting drunk, is a sin that carries its own punishment with it, and that a very severe one.'[22] Hannah saw through the emptiness of much of what happened in fashionable life, which held so many in its thrall. She wrote, 'The more I see of the "honoured, famed and great," the more I see of the littleness, the unsatisfactoriness of all created good; and that no earthly pleasure can fill up the wants of the immortal principle within.'[23]

The splendour of high society began to pall, however illustrious the company. Some years later she wrote:

> *I was at Lady Amherst's splendid assembly last week: dull and foolish as assemblies are, yet it is diverting to see them once or twice in a year. A noble suite of rooms, filled with 400 persons of the first rank, dressed in all the vanity which the present fantastic fashions allow: but alas! the eye is not satisfied with seeing and the ear has nothing to hear worth hearing. The Duke and Duchess of Cumberland came early: but the Prince of Wales did not arrive till near midnight. He was as usual all gaiety and gracefulness. He did me the honour to ask for me, and to tell me that he often wished to see me.*[24]

As the years went on Hannah was finding a growing incongruity between her increasing evangelical convictions ('the immortal principle within') and the social and theatrical world into which her success had admitted her. The truth seems to be that even by the time *Fatal Falsehood* was written, Hannah had in spirit deserted the stage for the pulpit. The overriding didactic aim of the play, 'a simple story of domestic woes', comes out clearly in her Preface.

For if to govern realms belongs to few,
Yet all who live have passions to subdue.
Self-conquest is the lesson books should preach,
Self-conquest is the theme the stage should teach.

In her old age Hannah regretted that she had ever written for the stage. When all her plays were republished in her *Collected Works*, she introduced them with a preface in which she denounced drama. But she never turned against Garrick. She wrote, 'Mr Garrick did a great deal towards its (the theatre's) purification. It is said not to have kept the ground it then gained.' Some five years passed between Garrick's death and Hannah's partial retirement to Cowslip Green, but her heart was no longer in the theatre and she was looking for a new sphere of work for her energies and gifts. Inwardly she feared that her best days were over. Little did she realize her life's work was just about to begin.

6

THE FLEDGLING
EVANGELICAL

Religion keeps her children in full employment.
It finds them work for every day in the week,
as well as on Sundays.

The Spirit of Prayer

The cottage at Cowslip Green is now a large country house in a
secluded lane just off the busy A38 Bristol to Bridgewater road.
There under the shadow of the Mendip Hills Hannah found rest
from 'the laborious trade' of visiting and assemblies. She occupied
herself with much gardening. She told her friend Mrs Boscawen:

*You will be glad to hear that I am comfortably established in
my little cottage. It is a pleasant wild place, and I am growing a
prodigious gardener, and make up by my industry for my want of
science. I work in it two or three hours every day; and by
the time the hour of visiting arrives, for even I have visitors in my
little corner, I am vastly glad of a pretence for sitting down.
I am rather proud of my pinks and roses.[1]*

Hannah was a genuine countrywoman with a love for the beauty
of the natural world. Her views to some extent anticipated the
new romanticism of the Wordsworths with its love for the simple
rustic life and its reaction against the growing industrialization of
England:

*It was worthy of the munificence of omnipotent Bounty, not
only to spread the earth with a rich profusion of whatever
is necessary and pleasant to animal life, but with whatever might*

55

invite to contemplative and intellectual life; not only to sustain but
to gratify; not only to nourish but to improve: by endless variety,
awakening curiosity, and by curiosity exciting research . . .
The mind . . . which is looking out for good, finds 'sermons in
stones, and good in everything.' To minds of an opposite
make, use destroys the effect, even if novelty had produced it. Little
habituated to reflection, they soon learn to behold a grove
of oaks with no higher feeling than a street of shops, and are as
little soothed with the murmurs of a rivulet, as with the
clatter of hackney coaches.[2]

She told Mr Pepys that she gardened in the morning and rode in
the evening 'through delicious lanes and hills', that she seldom
read and hardly wrote except the occasional letter. Hannah sought
to convert the 'silence and solitude into seasons of prayer' but she
was essentially an activist rather than a contemplative and found
that she would 'rather work for God than meditate upon him'.[3] Her
escape to the countryside was mirrored in the poem *Florio*, which
Hannah dedicated to Sir Horace Walpole. *Florio* is the story of a
feckless young man-about-town whose father has left him a fortune
on condition that he marry Celia, the daughter of a country squire.
Florio finds himself bored by life in the country and the plain food
served at Celia's table and runs back to his old life in London.
But the pleasures of town life soon pall and Florio returns to the
country and to roast mutton, to have his eyes opened to 'Nature's
all instructive book' and to claim the fair Celia as his bride.

Retirement from the glamour of London society to the bucolic
pleasures of rural Somerset was not without its conflicts for
Hannah. Part of her still craved for fame and splendour and
public recognition. But another part told herself that such self-
seeking was not consistent with her Christian faith. Something of
this struggle is reflected in what Hannah wrote some years later
about retirement:

To seek therefore a retreat till we have got rid of [this] ambition,
to fly to retirement as a scene of pleasure or improvement, till
the love of the world is eradicated from the heart; or at least
till this eradication is its predominant desire, will only conduct the
discontented mind to a long train of fresh disappointments, in
addition to that series of vexations of which it has so constantly
complained in the world.[4]

Hannah found that she was prepared for society but ill prepared for solitude. Peace was as elusive in the country as it was in the town if there was turmoil of soul within. And what were her motives in retirement?

> *We may deceive ourselves in this pursuit as we have done in others.*
> *We may fancy we are retiring from motives of religion, when*
> *we are only seeking a more agreeable mode of life. Or we may be*
> *flying from duty, when we fancy we are flying from temptation.*
> *We may flatter ourselves we are seeking the means of piety, when*
> *we are only running away from the perplexities of our situation;*
> *from trials which make, perhaps, a part of our duty . . . In*
> *retreating into the country for peace of mind, the temper you would*
> *find you must carry thither . . . If we retire upon the motive*
> *of 'Soul, take thine ease,' though neither covetousness nor sensuality*
> *be the promoting principle, if our object be a slothful indulgence,*
> *a retirement which does not involve benefit to others, as well*
> *as improvement to ourselves, we fail of the great purpose for which*
> *we came into the world, for which we withdraw from it . . .*
> *Religion is that motive yet quieting principle, which alone delivers*
> *a man from perturbation in the world and inanity in retirement;*
> *without it, he will in the one case be hurried into impetuosity, or in*
> *the other be sunk into stagnation. But religion long-neglected 'will*
> *not come when you do call for it.'*[5]

In the country Hannah found that time could easily be frittered away. Leisure gives easy opportunity for putting things off and 'business which may be done at any time is, for that very reason, not done at all'.[6] In solitude one has to learn to live with oneself. Surely Hannah was speaking of her own struggle for self-discipline over the vagaries of her own moods when she wrote:

> *If any one thinks that by retiring from the world, he shall get*
> *rid of his own evil tempers, solitude is the worst choice he could*
> *make . . . Many who live in the world have a mortified spirit,*
> *while others may bring to the cloister hearts overflowing with the*
> *love of that world from which it is easier to turn our faces*
> *than to withdraw our affections.*[7]

Hannah's much sought after solitude was short-lived. Once Hannah's rural retreat was discovered, it was invaded by an almost unceasing succession of visitors. Members of the nobility, bishops, poets and a host of others all made Cowslip Green a place of pilgrimage. Mrs Garrick visited her. The wealthy Mrs Montagu found it a great novelty to dine in a thatched cottage. William Wilberforce and his sister drove over from Bristol, and William brought his new bride. He was in poor health but high spirits and 'very much in love as ever you saw a poor gentleman'. Hannah told Mary Hamilton that she entertained the rector for tea in the root house and in the evenings walked in the moonlight with a little dog and two cats. But she had trouble with the farmer next door over his thorns and thistles and pigsties, and by his draining 'a certain edifice' into the boundary ditch. Hannah complained that she could no longer entertain her guests for tea because of objectionable sounds, sights and smells.

Hannah confided in her diary: 'So much company unspiritualises my mind and swallows up my time.'[8] But among those whose presence was always welcome were numbers of those Evangelical Anglicans who were to become known as the Clapham Sect. Hannah's continuing interest in the abolition of the slave trade and the education of the poor can be traced to her connection with these Christians where she found 'a hardy, serviceable and fruit-bearing and patrimonial religion'[9] after her own heart.

Hannah was a faithful churchwoman from childhood. She came to London with strict scruples about Sunday observance. Her growth in her commitment to evangelical principles came about in large measure as a result of her reading. Hannah was a diligent and wide reader. When staying at Hampton with the Garricks she would often read for four or five hours a day. At other times she would be laid up with severe headaches or what she described as rheumatism in the face. She read the Bible regularly and also books of sermons, equally devouring a Bible commentary by Matthew Henry or a book of philosophy by David Hume. She could explain Arianism, Socinianism and all the other 'isms' to Mrs Garrick. She wrote home from London in 1782:

> *I am up to my ears in books. I have just finished six*
> *volumes of Jortin's sermons; elegant but cold, and very low in*
> *doctrine, — 'plays around the head, but comes not to the heart.'*
> *Cardiphonia does; I like it much, though not every sentiment or*
> *expression it contains. I have almost gone through three very thick*
> *quartos of Mr Gibbon's History of the Lower Empire . . .*
> *Gibbon is a malignant painter, and though he does give the likeness*
> *of depraved Christianity, he magnifies deformities, and takes*

> *a profane delight in making the picture as hideous as he can . . . I am pleasantly engaged to spend the evening with (Virgil's) Aeneas.*[10]

The *Cardiphonia* to which Hannah referred was a work by the converted slave trader John Newton. Hannah was sent the book by Mrs Boscawen, and when she wrote to thank her she said, 'I like it prodigiously; it is full of vital, experimental religion.'[11] She was not acquainted with the author until she later went to hear John Newton preach from his pulpit at St Mary Woolnoth in the City of London. Afterwards she sat for an hour talking with Newton; when she returned home, her pockets were stuffed full of sermons. Newton introduced Hannah to other evangelical ministers and to the poetry of his friend William Cowper, best known today for his hymns. Hannah was overjoyed. 'I have found what I have been looking for all my life, a poet whom I can read on Sunday. I am enchanted with this poet.'[12]

From the first, the preacher and the poetess recognized an affinity of spirit. The two engaged in a regular correspondence chiefly on religious topics, and Newton became for Hannah a kind of father confessor to whom she could admit her weaknesses of spirit. She owed much to him for her interest in evangelical Christianity and in the abolition of the African slave trade, two subjects which increasingly absorbed her time and permeated her writings. With Garrick's death in 1779, followed by that of her own father at the beginning of 1783, Hannah became tired of the London world in which she was now a recognized figure. She still visited Eva Garrick in London and did the rounds of her friends: Mrs Walsingham at Thames Ditton, Mrs Montagu at Sandleford near Newbury, Mrs Kennicott in Oxford, Mrs Boscawen in Gloucestershire, Mrs Bouverie and Bishop Porteus in Kent. But despite her winter forays to London, her thoughts turned more and more to the rural retreat which she had built for herself in Somerset.

The 'thin walled cottage' was too damp for winter use, especially for one who suffered from chronic asthma and bronchitis. So Hannah spent the winter with her sisters, and continued her annual visits to London. At the end of 1789, the sisters sold their Bristol school. Selina Mills, a former pupil, announced in the *Bristol Journal* for 2 January 1790 that she proposed to continue the Misses More's boarding and day school for young ladies on exactly the same plan and with the same masters as before. Selina Mills ran the school until 1799 when she married Zachary Macaulay. On his return from the governorship of Sierra Leone, Macaulay had become a prominent member of the Clapham Sect and was active in the abolition of the slave trade and in the affairs of the Bible Society and the Church Missionary Society.

The More sisters moved to a newly built house in 76 Pulteney Street, Bath. Hannah detested Bath as a 'foolish, frivolous place'. It was too like London for her taste. But despite her protestations, Bath became her winter home for the next twelve years. Finding no evangelical Anglican church in Bath, Hannah, with her sisters, frequently attended evening worship at the Presbyterian church in Argyll Street, where William Jay was the minister. It should be noted that Hannah remained an Anglican on Sunday mornings, and that the Presbyterian service did not coincide with the times of Anglican worship. But nevertheless those who wished to attack Hannah's churchmanship never failed to cite her association with this dissenting conventicle, as nonconformist churches were then regarded.

But why did Hannah continue her annual trips to London? She wrote, 'I may cry out with Wolsey, "Vain pomp and glory of the world, I hate ye". He did not however renounce it while he could keep it and I am much in the same way.'[13] One reason Hannah continued to frequent London's fashionable society was that she had many friends there of whom she was genuinely fond. As she told John Newton, 'The world, though I live in the gay part of it, I do not actually much love; yet friendship and kindness have contributed to fix me there, and I dearly love many individuals in it.'[14] She also felt that her presence and influence could be used for the reformation of society. Dr Horne, who became Bishop of Norwich, told Hannah, 'We can tell people their duty from the pulpit; but you have the art to make them desirous of performing it, as their greatest pleasure and amusement.'[15]

When opportunity allowed, Hannah was keen to speak about her faith to some of her well-to-do acquaintances.

Lady B. and I had a long discourse yesterday; she seems anxious for religious information. I told her much plain truth, and she bore it so well, that I ventured to give her Doddridge . . . Miss — has also been with me several times — beautiful and accomplished; surrounded with flatterers and sunk in dissipation. I asked her

why she continued to live so much below, not only her principles,
but her understanding . . . did it make her happy? Happy, she
said, no; she was miserable. She despised the society she lived in,
and had no enjoyment of the pleasures in which her life was
consumed; but what could she do? She could not be singular — she
must do as her acquaintance did. I pushed it so home on her
conscience, that she wept bitterly, and embraced me. I conjured her
to read her Bible, with which she is utterly unacquainted. These
fine creatures are, I hope, sincere, when they promise to be better;
but the very next temptation that comes across them puts all
their good intentions to flight, and they go on, as if they had never
formed them; nay, all the worse for having formed and not realized
them. They shall have my prayers, which are the most effectual
part of our endeavours.[16]

Hannah had been genuinely shocked soon after coming to London
for the first time by the ostentation and extravagance of fashionable
society. It was with a desire to use her influence for good that she
brought out in 1788 her *Thoughts on the Importance of the Manners of
the Great to General Society*. This was followed in 1790 by *An
Estimate of the Religion of the Fashionable World*. Both books
were gentle attacks on the prevailing social customs and religious
practices of the day. As Hannah herself conceded, the books were
not at all profound. As a good Tory, she accepted the established
order in government and church, and the enormous differences of
wealth and privilege existing in England at the end of the eighteenth
century. Hannah contented herself by attacking the aristocracy for
their frivolity and for falsehoods, such as training servants to say
that their mistress was not at home when she was, and for fine ladies
calling for their hairdresser on a Sunday. She was furious to hear a
popular cleric tell his aristocratic congregation that they should be
extremely liberal in their charities as they were exempted from the
'severer virtues'. Hannah could not accept that there was one law
for the rich and another for the poor. Honesty, integrity, sobriety
and sabbath observance were the virtues that Hannah expected the
Great to observe so that they might permeate through all levels
of society. When we consider that these were the qualities that
Victorian England set so much store by, we may credit Hannah with
no small part in the shaping of nineteenth-century society.

Both *Manners of the Great* and *Religion of the Fashionable World* were published anonymously. But it was not long before people recognized Hannah's hand behind the books. She half expected to be ostracized for holding up the behaviour of her social superiors to criticism, and the success of the books must have surprised her. *Manners of the Great* went through seven editions in a few months, and the third edition was sold out in four hours. Hannah was flattered to hear that the Queen was sufficiently impressed with the work to stop summoning an outside hairdresser to attend to her on a Sunday. Horace Walpole, who liked to rib Hannah for her Puritanism, indulged in a little playful teasing of the author. He claimed that the Fourth Commandment was designed to give the labouring poor a rest on Sundays, and that it did not therefore apply to persons of fashion who needed no rest as they did nothing on the other six days of the week. But Hannah's friend, Bishop Beilby Porteus, was full of praise. He wrote to Hannah to take care of her health, 'for where . . . can we find any but yourself that can make the "fashionable world" read books of morality and religion, and find improvement when they are only looking for amusement?'[17]

7

THE NOBLE PATRON

Affliction is the school in which great virtues are
acquired, in which great characters are formed.
It is a kind of moral Gymnasium,
in which the disciples of Christ are trained
to robust exercise, hardy exertion,
and severe conflict.

Practical Piety

Anne Yearsley was a Bristol milkwoman, one of the band who
moved into the city in the early morning, balancing milk pails
on their low-crowned, broad-brimmed beaver hats and calling for
custom with cries of 'Hae any milk?' Having been raised from
provincial schoolmistress to London Bluestocking, it was quite
natural for Hannah More to consider it her duty to assist others
along the primrose path to fame. So when Hannah's cook first
introduced her to the poetry of Anne Yearsley, Hannah was in
no doubt as to her responsibility. Anne, the daughter of John and
Anne Cromarte, was born on Clifton Hill, Bristol, and baptized on
15 July 1752 at Clifton Parish Church. She married John Yearsley
in 1774 and bore him six children. The eldest son died and the
Yearsleys were rescued from near starvation by the benevolence of
the Vaughan family.

It was when Anne began calling at the Mores' kitchen to collect
scraps for her pig that she came to Hannah's attention. Hannah
read some of Anne's poetry and was amazed that one who had
had no formal education and had never even seen a dictionary
should display such talent. She immediately took Anne under her
wing and devoted the best part of thirteen months to teaching her
the rules of writing, spelling and composition, to transcribing and
correcting her poems, and to writing letters seeking subscribers.
Hannah reckoned that she wrote over one thousand pages on behalf

of the milkwoman.

Hannah's friends hastened to her assistance. Mrs Montagu, who thought Anne Yearsley to be 'one of nature's miracles', became a joint trustee with Hannah of the poet's fund. The subscription list eventually numbered over a thousand names and was headed by no fewer than nine duchesses. The fund raised over £600 and was invested in government stock to bring in a regular yearly income. With the sponsorship of this fund, Anne Yearsley's *Poems on Several Occasions* were published in June 1785. The poems were full of eulogies to Hannah as 'The Bright Instructress' and 'Soother of the Soul'. The Duchess of Beaufort and the Duchess of Rutland sent to meet this new poetic prodigy. Hannah told Mrs Boscawen, 'I hope all these honours will not turn her head and indispose her for her humble occupations . . . she will soon be the richest poetess, certainly the richest milkwoman in Great Britain.'[1]

These forebodings were sadly realized. Anne's success brought a fearful rupture with her patron. Mrs Montagu had warned that 'a legion of little demons: vanity, luxury, idleness, and pride, (might) enter the cottage the moment poverty vanished'.[2] The trouble arose over the trust deed which required Anne to renounce all the profits of her works to her trustees, Hannah and Mrs Montagu, to be invested at their discretion for the benefit of Anne and her children. Anne took umbrage and declared that she 'felt as a mother deemed unworthy of the tuition and care of her family'.[3] She spread rumours that Hannah was using the proceeds of the trust fund to buy herself an estate in the country, a wholly false allegation but one that was coloured by the fact that Hannah was in the process of buying herself the country cottage at Cowslip Green.

Hannah refused to modify the deed, which she considered to be in the best interests of one unused to fame and prosperity. She wrote to her friend Mrs Carter:

> *Prosperity is a great trial, and she could not stand it. I was afraid that it would turn her head, but I did not expect that it would harden her heart. I contrive to take the same care of her pecuniary interests, and am bringing out a second edition of her poems.*
> *My conscience tells me that I ought not to give up my trust for these poor children, on account of their mother's wickedness . . . I am grieved to take up your precious time with this mortifying story. It will not steel your heart, nor, I trust, mine against the next distress which may present itself to us; but there are many on whom I*

Hannah and Anne parted company for good. Bristol opinion was divided and Anne added further fuel by publishing a series of emotive pamphlets. Although she remained silent in public, Hannah was deeply hurt by what she felt to be Anne's ingratitude, but professed to feel only sorrow, not resentment, over one who could bear such hatred. Mrs Montagu and Hannah passed over their trusteeship to a Bristol lawyer. In course of time the trusteeship was assumed by a Bristol merchant, whom Anne finally persuaded to hand over all the fund monies. Anne used part of the money to apprentice a son to an engraver, and part to start a circulating library in Hotwells, Bristol. She brought out several more poems, a two volume novel, *Man in the Iron Mask*, and a play, *Earle Godwin*, which was acted in Bristol and Bath. But the milkwoman's hopes of fame and wealth were not forthcoming and she returned to relative obscurity, dying at Melksham in 1806 at the age of fifty-four.

It was Anne Yearsley who wrote about another remarkable character with whom Hannah came into contact about this time.

Beneath this stack Louisa's haystack rose.
Here the fair maniac bore three winter's snows.

Louisa, known as the Mad Maid of the Haystack, was discovered living in a haystack at Flax Bourton near Bristol by one of Mr Turner's relatives. The surrounding bushes were decorated with her trinkets. Described as beautiful but demented, she had been placed in St Peter's Hospital in Bristol, but was so miserable that she was allowed to return to her haystack, which was bought for her by a number of benevolent ladies. After Turner's cousin wrote to the More sisters, they visited Louisa and arranged for her to be placed in Mr Henderson's Asylum in Hanham, Bristol. The expenses were borne by the More sisters, Lord and Lady Bathurst and others of their wealthy friends.

Louisa's origins remain a mystery. She told an attendant that she had escaped with her lover from a convent in Schleswig, where she had been confined by her father for not marrying the bridegroom of his choosing. Gossip suggested that she might have been the illegitimate daughter of the Emperor Francis I. Hannah wrote her story in a halfpenny tract, *A Tale of Real Woe*, to raise money for her support. The tract casts no further light on Louisa's true identity. Louisa was visited at Hanham by John Wesley in 1782 and 1785. She died at Guy's Hospital, London, in 1801, supported to the end by Hannah and her sisters.

John Henderson was a brilliant student in whom Hannah took a personal interest. Sponsored by Dean Tucker and a number of wealthy Bristolians to go to Oxford, he showed signs of great abilities and talked well, but he was idle, failed to study and generally disappointed his patrons. Another protégée, Harriet Hester, took up atheism and a lover, and although often promising to give them both up never managed to achieve this. It was a valuable lesson for Hannah's later work for her to discover that generosity and goodwill alone are not sufficient to bring true reformation of character to the beneficiaries.

8

THE INDIGNANT ABOLITIONIST

Think on the wretched negro chained in the
hold of a slave-ship! think seriously on (this),
and put pride into your prayer if you can.

The Spirit of Prayer

In 1787 Hannah More's good friend Beilby Porteus was appointed
Bishop of London. Hannah wrote to Mrs Carter:

> *I rejoice for many reasons, but for none more than that his
> ecclesiastical jurisdiction extending to the West Indies, will make
> him of infinite usefulness in the great object I have so much at
> heart, — the project to abolish the slave trade in Africa. This most
> important cause has much occupied my thoughts this summer;
> the young gentleman who has embarked in it with the zeal of an
> apostle, has been much with me, and engaged all my little interest,
> and all my affections in it. It is to be brought before Parliament
> in the Spring.*[1]

The young gentleman was William Wilberforce. Hannah was first
introduced to the anti-slavery cause at a dinner party in 1776.
There she met Captain Middleton and his wife. (Middleton rose
in the course of an eminent career to become an admiral and a
Member of Parliament. He was knighted as Sir Charles Middleton
and ennobled as Lord Barham, First Lord of the Admiralty, at the
time of Trafalgar.) At the same party she met a close friend of Mrs
Middleton's, Elizabeth Bouverie, at whose mansion, Barham Court,
at Teston near Maidstone, the Middletons spent their summers.
The Rector of Teston, the Reverend James Ramsay, had been a

naval chaplain with firsthand experience of the evils of the slave trade. Teston and the Middletons' London home became the joint centres for the crusade to ban the slave trade. Wilberforce, Pitt and others were invited there to discuss the cause. Hannah wrote to her sister:

> *The other day just as I was going to dinner, arrived Lady Middleton, saying I must at all events come away with her immediately to dine with Mr Wilberforce at her house. We had four or five hours of most confidential and instructive conversation, in which we discussed all the great objects of reform which they have in view.*[2]

Hannah, with her spiritual interest fuelled through her contact with John Newton, the former slave trader, became an enthusiastic supporter of the cause. She showed dinner guests Thomas Clarkson's plan of a slave ship. She urged her friends to buy Elizabeth Bouverie's portrait of a black boy, and she pressed for Southerne's tragedy, *Oroonoko* or *The Royal Slave*, to be played at Drury Lane. She quarrelled with Lord Monboddo about slavery when that eccentric peer sought to justify it on principle. She was later able to reduce him to tears with a story about the heroism of one poor black servant, recounted by a naval captain at Sir Charles Middleton's table. This captain had lost his ship in a storm. Two little boys were on board under the care of a negro servant. This servant tied the boys in a bag, put in some food, slung them across his shoulder, and put them into the boat. As he was himself about to get into the boat, the black servant was told it was full and it was either his life or the boys'. 'The exalted heroic negro did not hesitate a moment; very well, said he, give my duty to my master, and tell him I beg pardon for all my faults. And then . . . plunged to the bottom never to rise again, till the sea shall give up her dead.'[3]

As early as 1788 Hannah carried out her own boycott of West Indian sugar in her tea. This was a boycott that she sought to promote among her friends. Dr Horne, who was then President of Magdalen College, Oxford, wrote in February 1788:

> *My wife has been much disturbed about this business of the slave-trade; till, yesterday morning she consulted Mrs. Onslow, who was a native of one of our West Indian islands. She came home much comforted, with the hope that matters might not be quite*

so bad as they have been represented, and in the afternoon,
put into her tea the usual quantity of sugar. I have not yet ventured
to read your poem to her, because, as she knows you never
say the thing that is not, I am afraid it will be the occasion of
withdrawing one lump and diminishing the other.[4]

Bristol merchants were deeply embroiled in the triangular trade
with West Africa and the West Indies. Ships sailed from Bristol for
West Africa with trinkets and other goods which were exchanged
for slaves. These slaves were then transported like cattle across the
Atlantic, many dying in transit. In the West Indies the slaves were
put up for sale and, from the proceeds, the ships were reloaded
with sugar, molasses and rum for the homeward journey. Edward
Colston and other Bristolians made their fortune from this trade.
From 'my savage city', Hannah kept her friends informed of the
reports of Thomas Clarkson who patrolled the Bristol docks spying
on the extent of the slave trade. Clarkson had been destined for
holy orders but, after being ordained deacon in the Church of
England, he devoted himself to the slavery issue. In 1787 he joined
with Granville Sharp and William Wilberforce in forming a society
for the abolition of the slave trade. He spent much time visiting
British ports and collecting evidence for the campaign being led
by Wilberforce in Parliament.

Although the main horrors of the middle passage were hidden
from Bristolians, occasionally the traffic did intrude itself upon the
city. Once, on a Sunday morning in 1790, the congregations of the
city churches were startled to hear the bell and voice of the crier
offering the reward of a guinea for the return of an escaped negro
girl. Her master, it appears, was determined to return her to the
West Indies. Hannah wrote to Horace Walpole:

To my great grief and indignation, the poor trembling wretch
was dragged out from a hole in the top of a house, where she had
hid herself, and forced on board ship. Alas! I did not know it
till too late, or I would have run the risk of buying her, and made
you, and the rest of my humane, I had almost said human
friends, help me out if the cost had been considerable.[5]

When Wilberforce presented his resolutions in 1788 binding
Parliament at least to consider the subject, Hannah was ready
with her poem *The Slave Trade*. The poem sings the praise of

liberty and human rights. Yet Hannah is careful to contrast true liberty with 'mad liberty', 'that unlicensed monster of the crowd':

> Clamouring for peace, she rends the air with noise,
> And to reform a part, the whole destroys.
> Reviles oppression only to oppress,
> And in the act of murder, breathes redress.

Hannah's views rested on a strong sense of common humanity ('Hold, murderers hold! . . . Respect the passions you yourselves possess'), and on the essential equality of all people, whatever their colour, who bear God's 'sacred image'. This understanding was melded with a strong sympathetic imagination, which pictured something of the horror:

> Whene'er to Afric's shores I turn my eyes,
> Horrors of deepest, deadliest guilt arise;
> I see, by more than fancy's mirror shown,
> The burning village and the blazing town;
> See the dire victim torn from social life,
> The shrieking babe, the agonizing wife;
> She, wretch forlorn! is dragg'd by hostile hands,
> To distant tyrants sold, in distant lands!

> When the fierce sun darts vertical his beams,
> And thirst and hunger mix their wild extremes;
> When the sharp iron* wounds his inmost soul,
> And his strain'd eyes in burning anguish roll;
> Will the parch'd negro own, ere he expire,
> No pain in hunger, and no heat in fire?

Hannah was not uninformed about her subject and added her own footnote to the word 'iron':

> * This is not said figuratively. The writer of these lines has seen a complete set of chains, fitted to each separate limb of these unhappy innocent men; together with instruments for wrenching open the jaws, contrived with such ingenious cruelty as would gratify the tender mercies of an inquisitor.

What pained Hannah was that these atrocities were committed by so-called Christians against pagans. She protested that 'they are not Christians who infest (Africa's) shore', but are rather white savages ruled by lust of gold or lust of conquest. Whatever the distortions of human history, Hannah took comfort in a final judgment. The tyrant trader or conqueror had better beware:

> *Though erring fame may grace, though false renown*
> *His life may blazon, or his memory crown;*
> *Yet the last audit shall reverse the cause;*
> *And God shall vindicate his broken laws.*

In such a final judgement the advantage lay not with the oppressing 'Christian' but with the oppressed pagan:

> *On Him, who made thee what thou art, depend;*
> *He who withholds the means, accepts the end.*
> *Thy mental night the Saviour will not blame,*
> *He died for those who never heard his name.*
> *Not* thine *the reckoning of light abus'd,*
> *Knowledge disgraced and liberty misus'd;*
> *On* thee *no awful judge incens'd shall sit,*
> *For parts perverted and dishonour'd wit.*
> *Where ignorance will be found the safest plea,*
> *How many learn'd and wise shall envy* thee.

The poem ends with a call to Britain to assume the lead in promoting faith, liberty and human rights throughout the world.

> *Shall Britain, where the soul of freedom reigns,*
> *Forge chains for others she herself disdains?*
> *Forbid it, Heaven! O let the nations know*
> *The liberty she loves she will bestow;*
> *Not to herself the glorious gift confin'd,*
> *She spreads the blessing wide as human kind;*
> *And, scorning narrow views of time and place,*
> *Bids all be free in earth's extended space.*

Such sentiments would motivate the great missionary movement of the nineteenth century, and would fire David Livingstone and others to bring Christianity and civilization to Africa.

But despite the 'high commission from above' to raise the 'shining standard' of liberty in 'Afric's suffering clime', the great cause languished because of parliamentary obstructionism, public indifference and war with France. Wilberforce's abolition bill in

71

1791 was soundly defeated in the House of Commons by 163 votes to 88. As the war went on abolitionism became tainted with republicanism and Jacobinism. Clarkson retired from the fray in 1794, and there were no meetings of the abolition society between 1797 and 1804. While the issue was moribund, Hannah sought to keep the matter before the public in her *Cheap Repository Tracts*, where 'this slave business' was not allowed to be forgotten.

Hannah retained her keen interest in the slavery issue. In her book *The Spirit of Prayer* published in 1825 she showed her continuing concern for slaves along with other suffering peoples:

> *Whenever you are tempted to thank God that you are not like other men, let it be in comparing your own condition with that of the afflicted and bereaved among your own friends; compare yourself with the paralytic on his couch; with the blind beggar by the wayside; with the labourer in the mine: think on the wretch in the galleys; on the condemned in the dungeons of despotic governments. Above all think, — and this is the intolerable acme of sin in the inflicter, and of misery in the sufferer, — think on the wretched negro chained in the hold of a slave-ship! think seriously on these, and put pride into your prayer if you can. Think on these, not to triumph in your superiority, but to adore the undeserved mercy of God, in giving you blessings to which you have no higher claim, and let your praise for yourself be converted into prayer for them.*[6]

Wilberforce kept up his dogged advocacy of abolition in Parliament and his efforts were finally crowned with success in 1807 when Parliament passed his bill to outlaw the slave trade. By then humanitarianism had found common cause with the interests of English sugar planters anxious not to face competition from revived plantations in captured French colonies. Both Wilberforce and Hannah were to live just long enough to witness the abolition of slavery throughout the British empire in 1833. Meanwhile Wilberforce was to be the means of calling Hannah to undertake another cause which was to occupy most of her remaining days.

9
THE MENDIP REFORMER

A religion which is all brain, and no heart,
is not the religion of the Gospel.

Christian Morals

At supper one evening Wilberforce unburdened his heart. He had seen the sights of Cheddar and the horrors of rural poverty. He said to Hannah:

> *Miss Hannah More. Something must be done for Cheddar. If you will be at the trouble I will be at the expense.*[1]

So began the 'trouble' which was to occupy Hannah and her sisters for the greater part of their remaining years. Thus it was to be a cause much nearer home than the African slave trade for which Hannah could justly blame Wilberforce for the greatest disturbance of her rural retirement. Hannah first met the young Member of Parliament in the autumn of 1787. She was immediately attracted by his combination of urbane charm and evangelical fervour. She admired his eloquence and was happily surprised that Wilberforce had 'as much wit as if he had no piety'.[2] Two years later, in August 1789, Wilberforce and his sister visited Cowslip Green. The More sisters pressed Wilberforce to take himself off to see the glories of the Cheddar Gorge. He returned, the cold chicken and wine for his lunch untouched in his carriage, his mind full not of natural beauty but of the human miseries that he had encountered. When Wilberforce issued his challenge to Hannah, her sister Patty records that 'something commonly called an impulse crossed my heart which told me that it was God's work, and would do'.[3]

The Mendip Scheme which the sisters conceived and developed was a comprehensive programme of elementary education, religious instruction, industrial and domestic training and social welfare. Charity schools endowed by private benefactors, such as that in Stapleton where Jacob More had taught, existed in various parts of the Kingdom, but none in the Mendips. Hannah had met both Robert Raikes of Gloucester and Sarah Trimmer of Brentford, who in their different ways pioneered the establishment of Sunday schools, which by 1786 were teaching some 200,000 children in England. Sunday schools already existed in Wrington and Churchill, but the Mendip Scheme was bolder and broader than a Sunday school venture. As Arthur Roberts, the editor of *Mendip Annals*, observed, the idea of educating the poor, particularly on a weekly basis, was a novel idea in those days. To use Wilberforce's own simile, the More sisters were the mainspring of the machine in this pioneering work.

The sisters' visits to the houses of the Mendip villagers opened their eyes to a poverty and ignorance beyond their imagining. They found whole families, 'father, mother, and up to four children' all sleeping in one bed. They were amazed at the patient endurance of the country folk with their grinding poverty, 'while the manufacturers who get twice their wages are rioting'.[4] Hannah More was horrified at conditions in the poor-houses. 'Mansions of misery', she called them. She wrote, 'I believe I see more misery in a week than some people believe exists in the whole world.'[5] She wrote to Members of Parliament, but found them too busy or too indifferent. So Hannah turned to some practical schemes of self-help.

In the Greater Schools, which were established at Cheddar, Shipham and Nailsea, the full scope of the Mendip Scheme operated with varying degrees of success. During the week the schoolmaster or schoolmistress was employed to give industrial, agricultural or domestic training to the village boys and girls. For a small fee, the farmers' sons were also instructed in the basic skills of reading, writing and arithmetic. On the Lord's Day a Sunday school was held for all the children in the district. The Sunday schools afforded an opportunity for the poorer children to learn reading as well as the Scriptures. Reading classes were held during the week for adolescents and young adults.

Alongside these educational efforts the sisters formed Women's Friendly Societies. In return for a small subscription, these welfare clubs offered benefits in times of sickness, maternity, and funerals. In addition the women were given religious and moral instruction, and hints on housekeeping and homecraft. Young brides were advised to invest their wedding portion on a teaspoon or a bit of plate. At the anniversary tea the sisters lectured the women on the state of the village, on whether church attendance had increased or not, and whether crime, swearing, scolding and sabbath-breaking had gone up or down. Those who had got married during the year received special gifts.[6]

The highlight of the work was the annual Mendip Feasts. The schoolchildren, their parents and the women of the Friendly Societies (dressed in smart linen gowns with new finery made specially for the occasion) would gather for a day out on the Mendip Hills. Patty desribes the first of these Feasts:

On the 4th of August, on Callow Hill, a high part of Mendip, all our children were assembled (except the new schools . . .). We left Cowslip Green in the morning with some friends, mounted in a waggon, dressed out with greens, flowers, &c. Another followed with the servants, thirteen large pieces of beef, forty-five great plum puddings, six hundred cakes, several loaves, and a great cask of cider . . . At the sound of a horn the procession began. A boy of the best character carried a little flag; we walked next, then Ma'am Baber, followed by the Cheddar children, and so on according to seniority; all the schools, one after another singing psalms. Upwards of four thousand people were assembled to see this interesting sight. After marching around our little railing, all were seated in pairs as they walked. The dinner was then carved, and each child had laid at his feet a large slice of beef, another of plum-pudding and a cake. The instant they were served, all arose, and six clergymen, who were present, said grace. All were again seated, and were permitted to eat as much as their stomachs would hold, and talk as fast as their tongues would go. When the children were properly feasted . . . some little examination into their acquirements took place. One girl could repeat twenty-four chapters, another fifteen; and many questions were put to them, which were answered to the satisfaction of the company, and to the credit of the children. As the design of the day was to prove to them the possibility of being merry and wise, we all joined in singing

"God save the King", and amused them with a little mirthful chat.
At four o'clock the pleasure was over, and the children marched out
of the circle in the order they entered, each school headed by
their master and mistress, singing psalms and hallelujahs, till they
were lost in the valley. Thus were five hundred and seventeen
children, and three hundred others, made happy, and really feasted
for the sum of £15.[7]

A special feature of the Feasts became the annual charge given
by Hannah herself. In her charge of 1793, Hannah began by
pointing to the transformation that had come over the children,
no longer half-naked and ignorant, given to idleness, swearing
and gaming. Now they were to be found 'at school, at prayer, at
church — serving the Lord, keeping his commandments, decently
clothed, creditable'.[8] But Hannah spoke sternly to the parents
about sending their children late to school, and admonished them
to be humble enough to learn from their children who could read
and explain the Bible to them. Warnings were also given about the
perils of dancing and going to lewd plays, which were regarded
as licentious affairs and a prelude to all kinds of immorality.
She urged the importance of keeping the sabbath and not going
to the shops on a Sunday. Godliness, cleanliness, decency and
the regular application of Christianity to everyday life were the
prevailing themes of the charges.

By modern standards the educational principles which motivated
Hannah More seem narrow and paternalistic. But her work must
not be judged by the standards of the end of the twentieth
century but by those of two centuries earlier. Hannah accepted
the hierarchical structure of society as divinely ordered. Indeed
she could see no alternative to it but the chaos and tyranny
manifested in the French Revolution. Initially she had rejoiced in
the destruction of the Bastille, which together with the Inquisition
and the African slave trade she saw as three great engines of the
Devil to be 'crushed, demolished and exterminated'.[9] But the
excesses of the French mob soon horrified her. As she wrote to
Horace Walpole, 'I can figure to myself no greater mischiefs than
despotism and popery, except anarchy and atheism.'[10]

Hannah made no secret of the fact that her supreme aim was to
make Christians and not to disturb the existing order of society:

My plan for instructing the poor is very limited and strict. They
learn of weekdays such coarse works as may fit them for servants. I

*allow of no writing. My object has not been to teach dogmas
and opinions, but to form the lower class to habits of industry and
virtue. I know of no way of teaching morals but by infusing
principles of Christianity, nor of teaching Christianity without a
thorough knowledge of Scripture . . . For many years I have
given away annually near two hundred Bibles, Common Prayer-
books, and Testaments . . . In some parishes, where the poor
are numerous, and where there are no gentry to assist them, I have
instituted, with considerable expense to myself, Friendly Benefit
Societies for poor women, which have proved a great relief to the
sick and lying-in, especially in the late seasons of scarcity and
distress . . . To make good members of society (and this can only be
done by making good Christians) has been my aim . . . Principles,
and not opinions, are what I labour to give them.[11]*

As time went on Hannah became aware that the limits she had
set for her educational programme were coming under increasing
criticism. But she considered it cruelty and not kindness to educate
people above their station in life, and to arouse expectations among
the poorest children which she knew society would not be able to
satisfy. She could see no point in giving the Mendip children of
the labouring classes an academic education which would be of
no value in their employment as miners or farm-workers, nor
enhance their moral or religious behaviour. The sons of farmers
were to receive sufficient education in the three Rs to qualify them
to serve as constables, overseers, churchwardens, and jurymen.
While conscious that 'the ultra-educationists' despised her limits,
she told Sir William Pepys in 1821, 'I have exerted my feeble voice
to prevail on my few parliamentary friends, to steer the middle
way between the scylla of brutal ignorance, and the charybdis of
a literary education. The one is cruel, the other preposterous.'[12]

As a woman of compassion and sympathy she desired social
amelioration. This was to be achieved not by constitutional
innovation, but by each class of society performing the duty laid
on it by Providence. It was the task of the ruling classes to govern
and to employ their leisure and their wealth in extensive works of
benevolence and philanthropy. Merchants and farmers must keep
running the commerce and agriculture of the nation, providing such
honest employment and godly charity as their means allowed. It
fell to the masses of the populace to provide the labour for factory
and mine, farm and homestead, and to practise steadfast loyalty,

industry and frugality. In many ways Hannah's emphasis upon personal responsibility and private philanthropy mirrors much of the thinking of the New Right today. But Hannah would never have accepted the autonomy of personal choice or the supremacy of market values. She believed in a transcendent moral order, so that both private practice and public life must be founded upon biblical standards.

10
THE GREATER SCHOOLS

Those princes and commonwealths who would keep their
governments entire and uncorrupt, are, above all things, to have
a care of religion and its ceremonies, and to preserve them
in due veneration; for in the whole world there is not a greater
sign of imminent ruin, than when God and his worship are
despised.

Machiavelli, cited with approval by Hannah More in *Hints to a Young
Princess*

Within five or six weeks of Wilberforce's visit in the summer of
1789, Hannah and Patty went to see Cheddar for themselves. They
stayed in a local public house while they looked around, at first
totally at a loss as to what they should do. The genteel ladies
suffered severe cultural shock at the conditions which they saw.
Hannah wrote to Wilberforce that the farmers 'are as ignorant as
the beasts that perish, intoxicated every day before dinner, and
plunged into such vice that I begin to think London a virtuous
place'.[1] The village of two thousand people lived under the petty
tyranny of a dozen or so ignorant and hard-hearted farmers, 'as
insolent aristocrats as any *ci-devant* nobles of France'. The sisters
found that the biggest farmer of the area was opposed to religion as
a very dangerous thing which could be the ruin of agriculture. But
the sisters brought their natural charm into play by complimenting
the farmer on his wine and assuring him that no subscription
was necessary. The farmer withdrew his objection to their school
project. His wife, although described as 'a woman of loose morals',
soon became their friend and later a strong Christian.

Cheddar, like a dozen or so of the neighbouring villages, suffered
from the blight of non-resident clergy. No clergyman had lived in
the village for forty years. The sisters on their visits found only
one Bible in the parish, and that was used to prop a flowerpot.
The vicar was an absentee don at Oxford who enjoyed the

stipend of the living but employed a poor assistant curate to take services for him. The curate lived in Wells and did a round journey of twelve miles on horseback to take the Sunday morning service. Eight people at the morning service and twenty in the evening was a good congregation. There was no pastoral care and nobody to visit the sick; and children were often buried without a funeral service. The sisters found 'as much knowledge of Christ as in the interior of Africa'. They reflected ruefully on the fact that while Britain was sending out missionaries 'to our distant colonies, our own villages are perishing for want of instruction'.[2]

At her own expense Hannah took the lease of a house and garden for the schoolmistress for a seven-year term at a rent of six and a half guineas a year. The ox-house next door was given a new roof, floor and windows, and was made into a schoolhouse. Every house in the village was visited and a list made of the members and occupations of each household. The sisters called all the women with children upwards of six years to a meeting in the church. One hundred and twenty children were invited to attend the following Sunday, but some mothers refused to send their children unless they were paid, and others refused because they feared that the sisters would acquire power over the children and send them overseas. Hannah also hired a mother and daughter as schoolmistresses. Cheddar School opened on Sunday 25 October 1789 with many parents present for the reading of portions of Scripture, part of the 34th Psalm, the singing of a hymn, and the reading of a specially composed prayer. The children were taken to church to hear a sermon by the curate on the laws of the land and the divine right of kings. A weekly school was established for thirty girls to learn reading, sewing, knitting and spinning.

At the end of a year, Hannah took to reading a sermon to a few invited parents and older children. The sisters began distributing Bibles, Prayer Books and other books to villagers who showed interest. Some of the parents began to meet on Wednesday nights during the winter to read the Scriptures, and some twenty or thirty young people started meeting on Tuesday nights for a similar purpose. There was some opposition to these activities which were branded as 'methodistical' and the school suffered several broken windows, but the sisters were not daunted. Hannah wrote encouragingly:

> *We have a great number there who could only tell their letters when they began, and can already read the Testament, and not only say the Catechism, but give pertinent answers to any questions which involve the first principles of Christianity.*[3]

Not only was Hannah concerned about the spiritual care of her villagers, but she took a lively and practical interest in their material welfare as well. Finding the wages pitifully low at one shilling per day, she set up credit clubs or societies for the women. In return for a weekly subscription of a penny-halfpenny, the women received three shillings a week when sick and seven shillings and sixpence a week when lying-in during childbirth. She wanted to train the women in spinning wool and she found a businessman who she hoped would buy woollen stockings made by them. She wrote to Mr Wilberforce:

> *With my usual bias in favour of this world, I have been diligent about the manufactory, and negligent of the mission . . . I find that spinning linen is a starving employment: a woman must add great skill to great industry, to get one shilling and sixpence per week; whereas the same exertions will enable her to get near three shillings by spinning wool. Now it strikes me that it would be profitable and pleasant, if they could be taught to spin the worsted for their own knitting . . . I think if we give them the wheels, their instruction, and a certain proportion of yarn to waste till they have acquired the art perfectly, — then the manufacturer should be the employer: I mean he should find the wool, pay for the spinning, and take the yarn or the stockings at a certain price . . . I can get wheels for spinning wool for about four shillings and sixpence each.*[4]

The Cheddar Friendly Benefit Society raised a fund of nearly £300, a substantial sum for those days, which Hannah prudently invested in government stocks. The fund was also increased by a legacy from the lady of the manor to the women's club and the school, in testimony of her good opinion of Hannah's work. Every young woman who passed through the school and the club, who had a testimonial of good conduct from the parish minister, and who had married during the year, was presented at the club's anniversary feast with five shillings, a pair of white stockings, knitted by Hannah herself, and a handsome Bible.

Later under the management of Mrs Baber, Cheddar became

81

the ideal school. Its Sunday school roll increased from 100 to 200 between 1791 and 1795, and the evening reading class reached 150 in summer and 200 in winter. On Sunday evenings school parents were induced to come for instruction in the foundations of religion. A new curate, Mr Boake, a 'very amiable and active young man', gave the school his whole-hearted encouragement. When Mrs Baber died in 1795 the whole village turned out to mourn her passing. Patty described it in her journal in a passage which E.M. Forster judged to be a masterpiece of macabre literature:

> *Her two hundred children followed the corpse, then the people; but what rendered it particularly affecting was, every creature had on some little badge of mourning, according as their little pence could be spared. The better sort of people in handsome mourning. Mr Boake attended from the house, which was esteemed a mark of great respect. The procession was immensely long, solemn and affecting; no noisy, clamorous grief, but a quiet, silent sorrow; the footsteps scarcely heard, and the tears running down their poor faces to the ground, their little ragged pocket handkerchiefs not being large enough to contain them. The church, on our entrance, appeared already full . . . When the last solemn office was performed, and "ashes to ashes, dust to dust" was pronounced, the people threw in their nosegays — it was the prettiest, most affecting little trait imaginable. The whole concluded with a suitable hymn, sung, or rather sobbed, by the children. For a long time there was no getting the people or children from the grave — a last look was the desire of every eye. The undertaker, usually callous by profession, wept like a child. (She added in a letter to Hannah, 'He confessed that, without emolument, it was worth going a hundred miles to see such a sight.')[5]*

Under Mrs Baber's influence 'this seemingly forgotten people, buried as it were in their own cliffs', were turned into 'an enlightened race'. 'Here the great work evidently goes on — the people hunger and thirst — the church is filled — families pray — children are easily brought to the knowledge of God — and, as a proof of their sincerity, are the means of being permitted to bring their parents.'[6] Such was the success of Hannah More's work at Cheddar that within a decade weekly church attendance in the parish had risen from fifty to seven hundred, and the number of communicants from fifteen to one hundred and twenty.

Similar success was to mark the sisters' efforts at Shipham. This village was almost wholly dependent upon the mining of calamine (zinc), which even today causes anxiety in the area as a possible health hazard. One writer likened the appearance of the miners going in and out of their mines to that of rabbits popping in and out of their burrows.[7] Shipham was notorious for the fierce independence of its people. 'No constable,' reported Patty in her journal, 'would venture to arrest a Shipham man, lest he should be concealed in one of their pits and never heard of more; no uncommon case.'[8] This reputation did not deter the intrepid More sisters. They were pleased to find that although the rector had never catechized a child or preached a sermon for forty years, the village was not without Christian witness.

Hannah and Patty mounted their horses and went in search of a poor farmer's daughter, Patience Seward, whom they found milking her cow. This girl on her own initiative had started a Sunday school of some thirty children. Patience and her half-sister, Flower Waite, together with two men, were engaged as schoolteachers for the new More school, opened in September 1790 in the derelict rectory which the rector was persuaded to put into repair. One hundred and forty children from Shipham and Rowberrow joined the school. Matters improved greatly when the curate, later known throughout the Mendips as Jones of Shipham, and 'truly Evangelical' in doctrine, was inducted into the living. By 1796 every house in the parish sent children to the school, and Hannah reported to Wilberforce that she had met two poor women who had been taught to read the Bible by their ten-year-old daughters.

At Shipham as at Cheddar, Hannah started a benefit club for the women. Patty describes in her journal the visit to the club in 1793:

We began to get ready for the Shipham Club, to the no small joy of the women, who were busy in preparing finery. We met a large body at three o'clock, and formed a most creditable procession to the church, where Mr Jones preached a useful, proper sermon. The bells were ringing for our arrival, and a rustic band of music preceded us all round the hill, to the great amusement of the numerous spectators . . . Two modest-looking brides came forward, and received the marriage portion, promised in the articles, of five shillings, a pair of worsted stockings of our own knitting, and a Bible. This was a very merry part of the feast; every one busy in advising the brides how to dispose of the wedding portion;

83

*every one dissuading them from eating it, but counselling them
to buy a teaspoon or some bit of plate. We have always accustomed
ourselves to give some little sort of exhortation . . . Some one has
wittily called it a* charge. *Our day, as usual, concluded with one
of these. The vices or faults particularly alluded to this year were
neglect of sending the children sufficiently early, going to shops
on Sundays, and not always telling the truth. The commendations
given were on the ground of the children being kept cleaner,
and made more civil.9*

Shipham was the scene of some of Hannah's most notable efforts
in practical philanthropy. In 1792 the village suffered from a
raging fever. Seven people died in two days including several of
the schoolchildren. Hannah wrote:

*Figure to yourself such a visitation in a place where a single cup of
broth cannot be obtained; for there is none to give, if it would save
life. I am ashamed of* my *comforts when I think of their wants;
one widow, to whom we allow a little pension, burnt her only table
for firing; another, one of her three chairs. I had the comfort,
however, of knowing that poor Jones distributed what we sent most
conscientiously, and ran the risk of walking into the pits with
which the place abounds, and which were so covered by snow that
he was near being lost. 'No words,' he wrote me, 'could describe
the sensations of this poor village at seeing a waggon-load of coal
we sent, enter the place!' I feel indignant to think that so small sum
can create such feelings, when one knows what sums one has
wasted. Most providentially we had a most respectable mistress at
the school, who entered so tenderly into their wants, that they
would send to fetch her at midnight, and she supplied all the sick
with broth, medicine etc.10*

Some years later, in the slump of calamine mining in 1817, Hannah
More and her friend and neighbour, Hiley Addington, acted as
merchants and with their private means bought up some of the
ore to store until better times returned — proof again, if such be
needed, that there was no division in Hannah's mind between the
Gospel and social action. Hannah took comfort in the remarkable
change that had come over in Shipham in the twenty-seven years
that she had run her school there. As she told Wilberforce:

*These poor people, who have often not tasted food more than
once in two days, have never uttered a word against Providence or*

government. A friend of mine called on one poor woman, who
was nearly famished, and asked her how she bore up. 'Madam,'
said she, 'when I feel very faint I go up and pray two or
three times a day, and I come down so refreshed.' How many fare
sumptuously every day, and never pray at all.[11]

Nailsea, the third of the Greater Schools, was then an isolated
community specializing in mining and glass-making. When the
sisters visited the glass house they described a scene more akin to
Dante's *Inferno* than Somerset rusticity. 'The high buildings of the
glass-houses ranged before the doors of these cottages — the great
furnaces roaring — the swearing, eating and drinking of these half-
dressed, black-looking beings, gave it a most infernal and horrible
appearance.'[12] The ladies were accompanied by a gentleman who
was too fearful to go with them among the inhabitants of this
rural slum. The glass people lived in nineteen little hovels in a
row containing nearly 200 people. The sisters entered each of these
homes, where they were politely received and made welcome to
'Botany Bay' and 'Little Hell' and so on, as the people called their
dwellings.

In Nailsea the farming heads of the parish, generally antagonistic
elsewhere, received the More sisters enthusiastically and offered to
erect a schoolhouse for them. The meeting was recorded in the
vestry minutes of 19 September 1791:

It was agreed to build a schoolhouse for the Master and Mistress of
Miss More's, standing upon a piece of ground given by Mrs
Baddily, adjoining to the school already built, and to put the stable
below into the order of a school for teaching, as is that above.[13]

In the presence of the local dignitaries in their best clothes, Hannah
laid the foundation stone over an inscription with these words:

September 30th, 1791
With an humble reliance on the
Blessing of Almighty God,
This little building was begun
With a sincere desire
To promote his glory,
To benefit the Parish of Nailsea
In its most important interest,

The educating of the rising generation,
In the knowledge and practice
of the Christian religion

Early in February 1792 Hannah and Patty More came to Nailsea to open the school. The roads were almost impassable owing to a heavy fall of snow, but they were warmly received with much rejoicing throughout the village and by the ringing of the church bells. A married couple, Mr and Mrs Younge from Bath, 'well recommended for religious zeal and industry', were imported to run the school. Patty found the children sharp and quick to learn. Within twenty-two weeks a large number could read the Bible fluently and some were beginning to understand it and learn from it. The school flourished as did the evening reading class.

When some of the pupils marched to Bristol to join in the strike of Somerset and Gloucestershire miners to raise the weekly wage from ten to twelve shillings, the sisters greeted their return with joy. 'It would create a smile in a fine gentleman or lady to behold our mutual pleasure on meeting; it was something quite transporting.'[14] All continued well in Nailsea until a dispute between the Younges and the heads of the parish, whom Patty now described as 'remarkably disagreeable, obstinate and ignorant, giving no encouragement to great boys and girls to attend'.[15] In 1795 the sisters reluctantly agreed to move the Younges to Blagdon, little realizing that this would provoke a much greater controversy.

A collier, John Haskins, was appointed to run the school until he was severely injured when a pit collapsed on him. His two assistants, Tommy Jones and Johnny Hart, also colliers, took over the the school from him. Patty records her satisfaction with their work:

A Higher Power not only presided over, but greatly blessed these two poor youths, who are concealed from all human sight in the bowels of the earth six days out of seven, and on the seventh they emerge, like two young apostles, to instruct and enlighten the rising generation, with a cheerfulness, humility and spirituality, that is necessary to be seen to be believed and fully comprehended; and we can with truth assert that we have no teachers of any age that excel them.[16]

The sisters made it a practice to take their meals with these young colliers. Hannah noted with amusement in her diary for Sunday 10 June 1796: 'How varied is my life: on Thursday dining with the Prince-Bishop of Durham — on Sunday with two religious colliers.'[17] By 1800 Patty's journal reported, 'We found Nailsea this year most prosperous indeed; our two young colliers active, obedient, zealous; the school full, the heads all attention and civility.'[18]

11

THE LESSER SCHOOLS

If . . . some children may hereafter,
in the hours of sorrow and distress,
recall to mind one useful sentence,
or recollect some text of Scripture
learned and explained at the school,
surely it has not been carried on for nought.

Patty More in *Mendip Annals*

The Lesser Schools, so called because they functioned only as Sunday schools and evening reading classes, were attended with very mixed results. The problem as Hannah More perceived it was one of supervision. The sisters found it increasingly difficult to supervise the effective running of their day and Sunday schools as the number of schools and pupils increased, and when the schools were scattered over an extensive area of the Mendip countryside.

The Sunday School at Sandford (a hamlet in Winscombe Parish) foundered after a promising beginning when the mistress, forced to give up through ill health, could not be replaced. At Banwell the schoolmistress struggled against the opposition of 'the rich, frigid farmers', who in due course were won round to provide a feast for the poor ragged children where they gave the boys handsome blue coats and the girls shawls. But the parents there showed no great interest in the school except to send their crying babies, and the school had to close when the mistress left in 1799. At Congresbury, however, 'what is called the gentleman farmers sent their children to be educated with the very poor'. Patty describes the alteration that came upon these village tyrants:

To behold two great, ignorant farmers each Sunday sitting
the whole day with people they oppress and trample on during the

*week, listening to these poor children, and those who are not
quite brutes endeavouring to teach, and when we appear, bowing
to the earth, and teaching the children to be dutiful and
grateful! One gentleman at Congresbury, bursting with his wealth
and consequence, and purple with his daily bottle of port,
was so affected . . . that, in an unguarded moment of rapture, he
exclaimed, 'Every boy and girl that do mind what the ladies do
say I'll give twopence a-piece to!' This was a piece of
generosity unknown in the family before.[1]*

The school at Congresbury, 'long a trouble and an expense',[2] suffered from poor teachers and was finally closed in 1796. But the sisters took comfort in the fact that at least they had taught the children to read the Bible.

At Yatton Hannah and her sisters experienced a rare welcome with the church bells ringing, the gentry and clergy giving the school their full support and volunteering to collect money to clothe the children. There they made a particular friendship with a pious farmer, who brought seven sons to the Sunday school and who shortly afterwards lost his wife in childbirth. Later he led a long family procession in deep mourning up the nave of Yatton church, carrying the baby in his arms. The sisters were much encouraged that the father could testify not only that God had sustained him through his time of trial, but that notwithstanding everything he was able to praise God. However the teachers at Yatton failed, the numbers diminished and 'aversion to religion materially increased'. In 1800 the sisters transferred their endeavours from Yatton to Chew Magna, which being 'populous, ignorant and wicked' demanded their attention.[3]

Axbridge was described as a 'wretched, beggarly town' under 'an unfeeling hard-hearted Corporation', which spent the town's money in riotous living. The incumbent was said to be intoxicated about six times a week and 'very frequently to be prevented from preaching by two black eyes, honestly earned by fighting'.[4] However the presence of the admirable Mr Boake, curate of Cheddar but resident in Axbridge, encouraged the sisters to open the school. The school opened for a hundred 'poor, little, dirty, wretched-looking creatures, half starved amongst the voluptuous eating of this *ancient corporation*, as they style themselves'.[5] The early days of this school were auspicious. The children learned their catechism and were actually permitted to sing once in the church, and the corporation was generous enough to buy gingerbread for the children.

In Axbridge an evening sermon reading was held which attracted up to a hundred people, many of them 'smart, well-dressed young men and women'.[6] The very success of these meetings led to opposition. It became necessary to dismiss the 'deplorable teachers', no longer careful of the children's morals. Matters improved under Mrs Carrol, a respectable young widow, who worked a reformation in cleanliness and decency. But in 1799 the school was forced to close and the mistress was transferred to Wedmore.

Wedmore was the last of the schools to be established. It consisted of some seventeen hamlets and was the largest and most populous parish in the diocese. The village people, the curate and the Mores' religious friends clamoured for a school. The sisters were reluctant to take on such a big work at a distance of some fourteen miles from their home, but were finally persuaded to act. They encountered the customary opposition from the farmers. John Barrow, the richest farmer in the area, feared that a school would put an end to property and bring revolution. He did not want his ploughman to be wiser than he was. He wanted workmen, not saints. His wife was equally vocal. She declared that the poor were placed where they were by Providence and were intended to be servants and slaves. 'The lower class were fated to be poor, and ignorant and wicked; and that, as wise as we were, we could not alter what was *decreed*.'[7] Hannah, who could never accept this brand of political or religious determinism, pressed ahead, taking courage from the eagerness of the poor. The response was enthusiastic.

One creditable old woman threw her arms round a parcel of fine little creatures, and eagerly exclaimed with her eyes running over, 'Now my grandchildren will be taught the way to God.'[8]

There was a dramatic incident at Morning Prayer on the Sunday before the school opened. After the sermon the clerk read out a paper signed by John Barrow summoning all who were opposed to the school to meet at the church on the Friday. This was immediately followed by Hannah's clergyman friend, Mr Drewitt, rising to his feet and calling all parents and children to meet for the opening of the school on the next Sunday. Patty recorded that

91

these two contradictory notices caused great consternation. 'The poor feared, the rich smiled.'[9] Despite all Barrow's blusterings and threats, however, he failed to get a single signature to his petition. At the Friday meeting:

> *This lordly savage called first upon a person on whose estate he had a considerable mortgage, and with all the impudence of wealth, in vulgar language ordered him to sign. His reply was, 'Mr. Barrow, though I am much in your power, yet I am still a man,' and refused his name.*[10]

Wedmore school opened under a schoolmaster called Harvon, or Harvard, who was active and moral, but rash and indiscreet. He soon managed to incur the displeasure of the heads of the parish, who petitioned the patron, the Dean of Wells, for his dismissal. He was accused of calling the bishops 'dumb dogs', with threatening hell fire against those who did not come to school and with distributing *A Guide to Methodism*. Patty complained with some irony that Hannah was obliged to write to the Dean and other high powers 'and use all her influence to enable us to go twenty-eight miles of a Sunday, instruct their poor, and spend seventy pounds a year upon them'.[11] Hannah lamented that Wedmore would prefer 'a Mahometan to a Methodist'. When Harvard's removal became unavoidable, he was replaced by Mrs Carrol from Axbridge. There was some improvement in the situation, but the last we hear in Patty's journal is that 'the parish [is] depraved and shocking as ever'.[12] But there were encouragements so that by 1796 Hannah was able to report to John Newton that her schools and societies had a total enrolment of between 1600 and 1700 in ten parishes.[13]

In addition to her Sunday school work, Hannah attempted to introduce some religion into the local poorhouses. At Wrington, Rowberrow, Churchill and Winscombe she found people to read morning and evening prayers in the poorhouses. But at Shipham nobody could be found who could read, although Hannah noted that 'every one could, and did, swear'.[14] At Nailsea Hannah was gratified to hear the testimony of one old man who had been awakened to religion by the reading of the prayers, and who exclaimed, 'Oh, ladies, your coming into this country has been the means of saving my soul.'[15]

From a twentieth-century viewpoint the aims of the More schools seem strictly limited and their curriculum very narrow. But the schools must be judged by the standards of their own day. They unquestionably broke new ground for the rural poor and they fulfilled their overarching purpose to instruct children in the Christian faith. Thus Scripture underlay all the teaching in the schools:

> *The grand subject of instruction with me is the Bible itself . . .*
> *To infuse a large quantity of Scripture into their minds, with plain*
> *practical comments in the way of conversation, is the means which*
> *I have found, under Providence, instrumental in forming the*
> *principles and directing the hearts of youth. God has promised His*
> blessing *on His* Word.[16]

In a letter to Mr Bowdler Hannah explained her teaching material:

> *In teaching in our Sunday-schools, the only books we use are*
> *two little tracts called 'Questions for the Mendip Schools,' . . . the*
> *Church Catechism (these are hung up in frames, half-a-dozen*
> *in a room), the Catechism broke (sic) into short questions, Spelling-*
> *books, Psalters, Common Prayer-book, and Bible. The little ones*
> *learn 'Watts' Hymns for Children' — they repeat the Collect every*
> *Sunday. In some of the schools a plain printed sermon and a*
> *printed prayer are read in the evening to the grown-up scholars and*
> *parents, and a psalm is sung.[17]*

What is remarkable is that Hannah continued her Sunday school work for some thirty years until forced to lay it down by old age and ill health. She never enjoyed good health. She often went for a week or so with what she described as nervous headaches. In 1793 she wrote that she was hardly ever without a cough and that the days with headaches were more frequent than those without. Her work would have been difficult enough for a person in robust health. The sisters travelled sometimes in appalling weather conditions, along roads and pathways frequently turned into mud-baths, to visit their schools. In 1791 Hannah apologized to John Newton for a delay in writing:

> *[I have] been a good deal indisposed by walking over our*
> *mountains late at night, which I was made to do by a*
> *frightful accident of a horse falling, but without doing me the least*
> *harm; — Not a bone of me was broken.[18]*

The sisters, whether on foot, horseback or carriage, were often out long and late. Hannah's diary for Sunday, 26 October 1794 records:

Visited Banwell, Sandford, Yatton, and read sermon at Shipham at night. The days are now short, and visits laborious and uncomfortable; and it is dark and late when we return. We are often out thirteen hours; yet the good providence of God has preserved us from evil, and gives us strength and faith to persevere.[19]

12
THE RELUCTANT
CONTROVERSIALIST

True resignation is the hardest lesson in the whole
school of Christ. It is the oftenest taught
and the latest learnt . . . The submission
of yesterday does not exonerate us
from the resignation of to-day.

The Spirit of Prayer

On the face of it, it was a quarrel between a headstrong,
opinionated woman and an arrogant, bigoted clergyman. But the
deeper issue concerned the supremacy of the established church
and the authority of its local minister. Everything had started
so promisingly at Blagdon, a place notorious for its crime and
litigation. The parish was at this time in a high state of excitement.
At the last assizes a local woman had been sentenced to death for
stealing butter, which had been offered for sale at a price she
thought unreasonable, and for attempting to riot. A deputation
from the parish consisting of the overseer and the churchwarden
waited upon the sisters and begged their help. They spoke of
the good that the school had done in the neighbouring parish of
Cheddar and of the lawlessness of their own parish. Patty wrote in
her journal:

> *Had the account been less interesting or solemn, our interview with
> these deputies would have been almost ridiculous. One of them, full
> six foot high, implored us with particular eagerness to come,
> because, he said, there were places where they were personally
> afraid to go. There is a little hamlet, called Charter House, on the
> top of Mendip, so wicked and lawless that they report thieving to
> have been handed down from father to son for the last forty years.
> The poor woman under sentence of death was an inhabitant of*

95

this place; and here it was that these tender hearted churchwardens
wished to send two nervous women, really for the above reason
of personal fear.[1]

The 'two nervous women', Hannah and Patty, plucked up courage
and in autumn 1795 opened the school at the express request of
this deputation and the curate, Mr Bere, who ran the parish in the
absence of the rector, Dr Crossman. Hannah reported the opening
to William Wilberforce:

> *This hot weather makes me suffer terribly, yet I have now and*
> *then a good day, and on Sunday was enabled to open the school.*
> *It was an affecting sight. Several of the grown-up youths had*
> *been tried at the last assizes; three were children of a person lately*
> *condemned to be hanged; — many thieves! all ignorant, profane*
> *and vicious beyond belief! Of this banditti we have enlisted one*
> *hundred and seventy; and when the clergyman, a hard man,*
> *who is also the magistrate, saw these creatures kneeling around us,*
> *whom he had seldom seen but to commit or punish in some*
> *way, he burst into tears.*[2]

The 170 pupils in the school ranged in age from eleven to twenty-
one years of age. Blagdon offered the village children instruction
to fit them to become overseers, constables, jurymen, farmers and
tradesmen. The school had an excellent beginning. In 1796, Patty's
journal noted 'Blagdon full and flourishing'. The following year she
reported that two quarter sessions and two assizes had passed
without any Blagdon person appearing in court and, 'moreover,
warrants for wood-stealing, pilfering, &c., are quite out of
fashion'.[3]

But the curate, Mr Bere, began to turn against the school.
In a sermon in 1798, he indirectly preached against it. The
schoolmaster retaliated by accusing Bere of holding Socinian
(unitarian) views on the Trinity. The parish was stirred up into
contending parties. The numbers at school dropped from two
hundred to thirty-five. The More sisters were roused to action
and called a large public meeting at which Hannah threatened
to remove the school if there was no improvement. One of
the religious farmers confessed that the people were scared of
offending the clergyman who, as a magistrate, ruled them with a
rod of iron. The clergyman himself met the sisters in a state of great
agitation. When shown the letters of approval for the school that he

had written, he was forced to admit the extraordinary benefits that the school had brought to the village. For the time being peace was restored and the school filled up again, but 'Satan was active'.

In 1800 'a violent explosion, long pent up, took place at Blagdon. The curate and justice no longer concealed the cloven foot.'[4] In an 'impudent' letter to Hannah, Bere curtly demanded the dismissal of Younge, the schoolmaster. Hannah, who was visiting London, referred the dispute to Sir Abraham Elton of Clevedon Court. Sir Abraham, who was both a clergyman and a magistrate, investigated the dispute and cleared the schoolmaster of Bere's accusations. But Bere, thoroughly up in arms, would not be placated. He made public his accusations against Younge: the schoolmaster had turned the evening reading classes into a private unlicensed conventicle, in which he had taught fiery Calvinistic doctrines at variance with the teaching of the Church of England. He had adopted the class discipline of the Methodists, encouraged extempore prayer, questioned pupils on their spiritual experiences and attacked the curate's character.[5] 'I mourn to see that nothing is thought a crime but that they are pleased to call enthusiasm. I heartily wish that I were a greater enthusiast in *their* sense of the word,' wrote Hannah to Wilberforce.[6]

For three years the battle raged with increasing acrimony and bitterness. Bere rounded up every malcontent in the district and persuaded them to swear affidavits against Hannah and her schools. These affidavits would never have been accepted in a court of law since they were sworn before Bere in his own cause. Both sides issued pamphlets. Notices on the turnpike road invited visitors to 'the menagerie of five female savages of the most desperate kind'. Nine local clergymen made a public statement defending the conduct of Miss More's schools. Edmund Spencer of Wells attacked the 'She-Bishop' and her clerical 'Ninepins', and accused Hannah of encouraging religious and political disaffection. Hannah was even accused of praying in her schools for the success of the French in the war against Britain. The controversy attracted the attention of the London press and journals. The *Anti-Jacobin Review*, a high Tory publication, hardly missed an issue without attacking Hannah.

Throughout all the public vilification Hannah maintained a dignified silence. The Lord Chancellor, Lord Loughborough, advised her to prosecute for libel, but she steadfastly refused to be drawn personally into the public controversy or to engage in litigation. But for Hannah it was a period of intense personal strain aggravated by an illness of some seven months of ague — a fever with hot and cold fits. 'This heavy blow . . . has almost bowed me to the ground.'[7] Under the assault of Bere's affidavits, 'plenty as blackberries', she confided to Wilberforce:

> *My dear friend, I have prayed and struggled earnestly not (sic)*
> *to be quite subdued in my mind — but I cannot command my*
> *nerves, and though pretty well during the bustle of the day, yet I*
> *get such agitated and disturbed nights, that I could not answer for*
> *my lasting if the thing were to go on much longer . . . 'How shall I*
> *give thee up Ephraim', is my frequent exclamation, as I walk*
> *in my garden, and look at the steeple, and the village of Blagdon.*[8]

Under pressure from Bere, Hannah eventually removed Younge and closed the school. Bere illuminated the rectory and rang the church bells. His triumph was short-lived since Dr Crossman, the rector, was prevailed upon by the Bishop to dismiss Bere. The curate was now the aggrieved party. But public opinion slowly swung behind Hannah, and the appointment in 1802 of Dr Richard Beadon as Bishop of Bath and Wells to succeed the aged and vacillating Dr Charles Moss brought matters to a conclusion. In a lengthy letter to the new bishop, Hannah defended her schools and denied the charges against her of Methodism and Calvinism. She insisted that she had not started one school without the co-operation of the local parish clergyman, and that church attendance was a necessary part of the schools' discipline. Finally she declared herself ready to close all her schools should the bishop so order.[9] In his reply, Dr Beadon stated that he had no doubts as to Hannah's faith or patriotism and wished the schools every success so long as they continued under Hannah's control and that of the local parish minister.[10]

At the root of the Blagdon controversy was a struggle for the souls and bodies of the labouring poor. The farming opponents of Hannah More claimed a monopoly over the labour of the poor, and resented any religious or educational influence which might weaken their control. A high churchman like Bere claimed a spiritual monopoly over his parishioners. Any religious instruction in the parish must be under his exclusive authority. No form of dissent, whether religious or political, could be tolerated. The supremacy of the established church was not to be surrendered. Furthermore, to such a cast of mind, religious enthusiasm was nothing but Methodism in disguise. Hannah was never a Methodist. She protested to Dr Beadon that she had never been to Lady Huntingdon's chapel in Bath nor to any of Whitefield's or Wesley's chapels in London. She was an orthodox churchwoman in the evangelical tradition. As she wrote in her diary for 8 July 1803:

> My very soul is sick of religious controversy. How I hate the little narrowing names of Arminian and Calvinist! Christianity is a broad basis. Bible Christianity is what I love; that does not insist on opinions indifferent in themselves; — a Christianity practical and pure, which teaches holiness, humility, repentance and faith in Christ; and which after summing up all the evangelical graces, declares that the greatest of these is charity.

Hannah's ecumenical spirit was well ahead of her times. Despite criticism she was quite happy to work with nonconformists, whatever their denominational label, provided they shared her love for the Jesus of scripture.[11]

13
THE CHRISTIAN MORALIST

Christianity and riches are deposited in the hands
of Christians, for the more general
dispersion of both to the respectively destitute.

The Spirit of Prayer

It might seem that the management of the Mendip schools and
the Friendly Societies would be sufficient occupation for a retired
middle-aged woman, whose health was indifferent to poor. Yet all
the time Hannah maintained a heavy routine of writing. From
her pen flowed an endless succession of letters, books, pamphlets
and tracts. As her religious convictions grew, Hannah devoted her
literary gifts increasingly to propagating her evangelical faith and
what she considered a scriptural view of manners, morals and
politics. Although Hannah's reputation as a writer did not long
survive her death, there can be no doubt as to her popularity and
influence in her own day. The very wide circulation of her works
is evidence of her effectiveness as a communicator and opinion
former.

Although the Wesleys were never closely associated with
Hannah, Charles did send her a message via Betty More: 'Tell
her to live in the world; there is the sphere of her usefulness;
they will not let us come nigh them.'[1] The world to which Wesley
referred was the aristocratic world of high society in which Hannah
had been such a star. She shared with Wilberforce a passionate
concern for the 'reformation of manners', by which they meant
the moral and religious uplift of the nation. After Hannah's
retreat to Cowslip Green she fired off a number of broadsides
addressed to the rich and powerful.[2] In the first, *Thoughts on the*

Importance of the Manners of the Great to General Society (1788), she addressed not the distinctly virtuous or wicked but the generality of the upper classes, persons not indisposed to religion or morality. These respectable persons of high rank were castigated for their lukewarmness and indifference to the things of the spirit, for their carelessness and thoughtlessness in matters of religion. They were accused of breaching the 'Palladium (the safeguard) of Christianity' by giving Sunday concerts and by employing hairdressers to tend elaborate coiffures on the Lord's Day. Masters and mistresses were guilty of dishonesty in instructing servants to tell unwelcome guests that they were 'not at home'. Polite conversation had abolished the difference between right and wrong, so that the gravest offences were spoken of with 'cool indifference' and 'toleration'. By their petty deceits and hypocrisies the outward upholders of Christianity were responsible for a graver disservice to true religion than its avowed detractors.

The *Manners* was published anonymously but its true authorship soon became public knowledge. Far from finding 'every door shut against her', Hannah was surprised at the book's favourable reception. The French Revolution caused a quickening of moral and religious interest. Frivolity went out of fashion and a new earnestness was evident. Ladies of rank, such as Countess Spencer and Lady Charlotte Wentworth, discussed religion with Miss More, and were advised to read the Bible and spiritual books like Doddridge's *Rise and Progress of Religion in the Soul*. Queen Charlotte set a royal example of sabbatarian rectitude by dismissing her hairdresser on a Sunday. Horace Walpole alone of Hannah's fashionable friends took her to task for her puritanical strictness.

Nor did Horace Walpole approve of Hannah's next book, *An Estimate of the Religion of the Fashionable World* (1790). Conscious that *Manners* could be interpreted as preaching morality and not the gospel, Hannah sought to redress the balance. Salvation was a matter of faith, not of benevolence or good works. True religion required a 'turning of the whole mind to God'. Hannah's unflattering estimate of fashionable religion made her enemies. One lady at a 'baby ball' (something of which Hannah strongly disapproved) provided a doll dressed as Hannah More and invited the children to show their resentment at the person who interfered with their enjoyment. But the *Estimate* opened the way to Hannah's long friendship with Her Royal Highness Maria, Duchess of Gloucester. This led to long religious conversations at

Gloucester House and readings of Paul's letter to the Ephesians from the Bible and Wilberforce's essay on 'Human Corruption'.

Although the nobility and gentility read Hannah More's books, they did not always heed her. Disappointed by their response, Hannah turned her attention to the lower end of the social stratum, the kind of people with whom she was coming into increasing contact through her work in the Mendips. She did, however, return to the upper classes in 1799 with her *Strictures on the Modern System of Education with a view of the Principles and Conduct Prevalent among Women of Rank and Fortune*. Based on the premise that the prime need was to 'awaken the drowsy spirit of religious principles', the *Strictures* sought to inculcate true religion, sound knowledge and self-discipline, in place of the craze for 'a frenzy of accomplishments' in dancing, music, novel-reading and the like. Education, Hannah insisted, must be founded on a proper understanding of Christian doctrine, especially human corruption and its redemption through the atoning work of Christ.

Strictures was intended to impress upon society the vital need for women to have a good education. Hannah thought it 'a singular injustice which is often exercised towards women, first to give them a defective education, and then to expect from them the most undeviating purity of conduct'.[3] Hannah believed that women exercised an enormous influence if it could but be acknowledged.

> *The general state of civilised society depends more than those*
> *are aware who are not accustomed to scrutinise into the springs of*
> *human action on the prevailing sentiments and habits of women,*
> *and on the nature and degree of the estimation in which they*
> *are held.*[4]

She considered that women's power over the desires and passions of men was well recognized, but this had been at the expense of their moral and intellectual power.

> *To use their boasted power over mankind to no higher purpose*
> *than the gratification of vanity or the indulgence of pleasure, is the*
> *degrading triumph to those fair victims to luxury, caprice and*
> *despotism, whom the laws and the religion of the voluptuous*
> *prophet of Arabia exclude from light, liberty and knowledge: and it*
> *is humbling to reflect, that in those countries in which the fondness*
> *for the mere persons of women is carried to the highest excess,*

103

they are slaves; and that their moral and intellectual degradation increases in direct proportion to the adoration which is paid to mere external charms.

So Hannah did battle with prevailing ideas of female education, which laid stress on outward artistic accomplishments, designed 'to allure and to shine', but gave rise to 'a thousand yet unborn vanities', and which would not stand the test of time unless 'safely erected on the broad and solid base of Christian humility'.[5] In contrast with education for show, Hannah urged that women be given a rounded education with wide reading in history, good literature, logic and the Christian religion. So she recommended that girls be encouraged after the necessary preparatory reading 'to swallow and digest such strong meat as Watt's or Duncan's little book on Logic, some parts of Mr Locke's Essay on the Human Understanding, and Bishop Butler's Analogy'.[6]

Hannah's views on the women of her time were not flattering. She thought that they were 'little accustomed to close reasoning on any subject . . . and this perhaps is one cause . . . of the too great confidence that they are disposed to place in their own opinions'.[7] She even concurred with what she called the 'just remark of Swift' that 'after all her boasted acquirements, a woman will, generally speaking, be found to possess less of what is called learning than a common school-boy'.[8] This is not an inverted form of male chauvinism but reflects Hannah's sincere concern to raise the standards of female education. Her aim was not to challenge a male dominated society, but to give women the highest intellectual equipment that they might exercise a sweetening and enlightening influence on the men to whom they were wives or mothers. She strongly believed in the differentiation of the sexes and in the different roles to which men and women were called. But she thought that women had particular qualities of intuition, of imagination, of memory and of taste and feeling. Furthermore she thought that it was unfair to judge between male and female intelligence until women received better education.

Till the female sex are more carefully instructed, this question will always remain undecided as to the degree *of difference between the masculine and feminine understandings, as the question between the understandings of blacks and whites; for until men and women, and until Africans and Europeans are put more nearly on a*

par in the cultivation of their minds, the shades of distinction,
whatever they be, between their native abilities can never be fairly
ascertained.[9]

All learning for Hannah must serve to inform and instruct the Christian in his or her advancement in faith and practical holiness. History and biography, for example, give a clearer insight into the corruption of human nature. Knowledge should be acquired not as an end in itself but to further self-awareness and self-knowledge. She insisted on accuracy in language both as an aid to effective communication and to further the cause of truth. She would not have had much sympathy with any attempt to be economical with the truth! Learning and life were inseparable, and that is why Hannah placed much stress on the early learning of good habits.

> *It can never be too often repeated that one of the great objects*
> *of education is the forming of habits . . . The forming of any good*
> *habit seems to be effected rather by avoiding the opposite habit,*
> *and by resisting every temptation to the opposite vice, than by the*
> *occasional practice of the virtue required.* Humility, *for instance, is*
> *less an act than a disposition of mind. It is not so much a*
> *single performance of some detached humble deed, as an incessant*
> *watchfulness against every propensity to pride.*[10]

The habits which Hannah wished to see formed in young ladies were sobriety, meekness, economy, punctuality and discerning judgment. But she especially stressed the need for what she called 'unremitting industry'.

> *The masters in science, the leaders in literature, legislators and*
> *statesmen, even apostles and reformers, would not, at least in*
> *so eminent a degree, have enlightened, converted and astonished the*
> *world, had they not been eminent possessors of this sober and*
> *unostentatious quality. It is this quality to which the immortal*
> *Newton modestly ascribed his own vast attainments; who, when he*
> *was asked by what means he had been enabled to make that*
> *successful progress which struck mankind with wonder, replied,*
> *that it was not so much owing to any superior strength of genius,*
> *as an habit of patient thinking, laborious attention, and close*
> *application.*[11]

Here we see Hannah aligning herself firmly with that Protestant work ethic which was to transform the undisciplined indulgence of Georgian England into the rigorous industry of Victoria's realm. The influence of women as wives and mothers in forming the ethos of this new industrious society would be incalculable. For Hannah the mainspring of this new society must be a lively religious faith. Religion must be taught from an early age not by dull rote but by dialogue, 'through animated conversation and lively discussion' and the use of apt illustrations, just as Jesus taught by parables.

> *There seems no good reason that while every other thing is to be made amusing, religion alone must be dull and uninviting . . . Why should not the most entertaining powers of the human mind be consecrated to that subject which is most worthy of their full exercise?[12]*

It would be a travesty to regard Hannah as a killjoy. She herself argued that 'piety maintains no natural war with elegance, and Christianity could be no gainer by making her disciples unamiable'.[13] It was because the fashionable trend towards dressing up young children for 'baby balls' robbed them of their childhood that she attacked the balls as 'a sort of triple conspiracy against the innocence, the health, and the happiness of children'.

> *They step at once from the nursery to the ballroom; and, by a change of habits as new as it is preposterous, are thinking of dressing themselves, at an age when they used to be dressing dolls. Instead of bounding with the unrestrained freedom of wood-nymphs over hill and dale, their cheeks flushed with health, and their hearts overflowing with happiness, these gay little creatures are shut up all the morning . . . transacting the serious business of acquiring a new step for the evening . . . The true pleasures of childhood are cheap and natural; for every object teems with delight to eyes and hearts new to the enjoyment of life; nay, the hearts of healthy children abound with a general disposition to mirth and joyfulness, even without a specific object to excite it . . . Only furnish them with a few simple and harmless materials, and a little, but not too much leisure, and they will manufacture their own pleasures with more skill, and success and satisfaction, than they will receive from all your money can purchase.[14]*

Here we see Hannah carried back in her mind's eye to happy days in the sisters' home in Fishponds and in the surrounding countryside. One doubts if she would have been impressed with today's television generation of children.

106

While childhood preserves its native simplicity, every little change
is interesting, every gratification a luxury. A ride or a walk,
a garland of flowers of her own forming, a plant of her own
cultivating, will be a delightful amusement to a child in her natural
state; but these harmless and interesting recreations will be dull
and tasteless to a sophisticated little creature, nursed in such forced,
and costly, and vapid pleasures.[15]

Young ladies born with the advantages of rank and wealth were
expected to conform to the highest moral standards. Privilege,
Hannah insisted, carried great responsibilities. Servants must
always be treated with politeness and consideration. The test
was whether the chambermaid was treated in the same manner
as the guest. Servants should never be disturbed during their times
for meals and rest save for overwhelming necessity. Time was a
sacred commodity to be guarded so that every moment should
be employed usefully and every talent consecrated to the service
of God. There was a special duty which the rich owed to the poor.

Young ladies should be accustomed to set apart a fixed part of
their time, as sacred to the poor, whether in relieving, instructing,
or working for them; and the performance of this duty must not
be left to the event of contingent circumstances, or the operation of
accidental impressions; but it must be established into a principle,
and wrought into a habit. A specific portion of the day must
be allotted to it, on which no common engagement must be allowed
to intrench.[16]

What Hannah was advocating was not occasional forays of
Lady Bountiful benevolence, but a consistent programme of
philanthropy. Such charity was not only as a Christian duty but
it also helped to soften the differences between rich and poor. She
urged the great and powerful:

Let them train up their children to supply by individual kindness
those cases of hardship which laws cannot reach; let them obviate,
by an active and well-directed compassion, those imperfections
of which the best constructed human institutions must unavoidably
partake; and, by the exercise of private bounty, early inculcated,
soften those distresses which can never come under the cognizance of
even the best government. Let them teach their offspring, that the
charity of the rich should ever be subsidiary to the public provision

107

in those numberless instances to which the most equal laws cannot apply.[17]

Hannah shared the modern view that public provision by the government plays a primary role in the relief of poverty, but she believed that it needed to be supplemented by private charity. Of course she could have had no comprehension of the welfare state, a twentieth-century invention that depends upon a higher degree of general affluence than could have been conceived possible at the end of the eighteenth century. It was a highly paternalistic policy that she espoused, for she had few other models of relief to guide her. She firmly rejected egalitarianism for several reasons. She believed that to take from the rich to pay the poor would only lead to the impoverishment of rich and poor alike. Furthermore Hannah, like the majority of her fellow countrymen, was horrified by the course of events in France where the revolution based on liberty, fraternity and equality had led to a bloody terror and finally military dictatorship.

Strictures went through at least nine editions in two years and sold 19,000 copies. The critics were generally favourable, the Bishop of London recommended the book in his charge to the clergy of his diocese, and the book was even read at court. This led Hannah six years later to write a book concerning the education of the nine-year-old Princess Charlotte Augusta, daughter of the Prince of Wales, and next in line to the throne after her father. *Hints Towards the Education of a Young Princess* (1805) followed a similar argument to that of *Strictures*. Hannah recommended that the royal pupil learn Latin, French and German, geography and history. The latter was especially important and should be read with a map. 'History is the glass by which the royal mind is dressed.'[18] Hannah herself displayed a considerable knowledge of ancient and European history in the two volumes of the work. But she saw little reason for the Princess to learn more than an outline of natural history, botany and other sciences. 'The royal personage must not be examining plants, when she should be studying laws; nor investigating the instincts of animals, when she should be analyzing the characters of men.'[19]

Hannah was particularly anxious that the Princess's education should be designed to produce Christian character. Volume II of the book contains a strong defence of the Reformation and the Church of England, which she saw as pursuing the middle road between ritualistic Lutheranism and austere Calvinism. She warned against the dangers of flattery from sycophants, and told the Princess that her royal pomp should induce humility and not haughtiness. The book was read to the child Princess who found that it made 'the hours so long'. Princess Charlotte read the book again on her eighteenth birthday, not long before her death in childbirth at the age of nineteen years. So died tragically the young girl who would otherwise have been Queen of England.

Strictures had seemed somewhat scornful of novels and novel-reading. It was therefore some surprise when Hannah in 1808 wrote a novel, *Coelebs*, her first and last. To some extent she had reconciled herself to the place of the novel, but her venture into this field was primarily didactic. Hannah had become aware of a vast new market in the circulating libraries, the subscribers to which were largely fed on an unedifying diet of romantic fiction. Coelebs, a well-bred young man, described by M.G. Jones as a 'totally uninteresting prig', goes in search of a wife, whom he eventually finds in Lucille Stanley, the epitome of feminine piety and goodness. The book was intended to offer the middle classes a guide to female propriety in relationships with the opposite sex. It also presented evangelicalism in a favourable light as the religion of the home. The novel, which is largely devoid of characterization or creative imagination, was savaged by Sidney Smith in the *Edinburgh Review*, but it proved very popular in Britain and America and over thirty thousand copies were sold. Its identification of evangelical religion with domestic contentment was to set the scene for the century just beginning. M.G. Jones' verdict, quoting Lady Chatterton, on Hannah is:

'By her strictly commonplace writings she calmed the religious apprehensions of a huge public, whose hearts were stronger than their heads'. By so doing she popularized Evangelicalism among the upper and middle classes, and thereby strengthened its influence.[20]

Hannah never attempted another novel. Her talents did not lie in fiction, although M.G. Jones reckons her a precursor of Jane Austen. Hannah's later writings were of a more distinctly religious character. To these writings we shall turn after looking at her efforts to reach a popular market for the Christian cause.

14
THE POPULAR PROPAGANDIST

Here, by red lightning struck to earth,
The bold blasphemer lies,
That mother smote who gave him birth,
And on HER grave he dies.

Ye children all, who view this sod,
Betimes learn well this truth:
To HONOR PARENTS, LOVE your GOD,
Now in your days of youth.

The Thunderstorm; or *The History of Tom Watson*

The French Revolution precipitated Hannah into what was to be her most intensive literary labour — writing for the new mass market. Her experience in the Mendip Schools had shown her that there was little popular literature of an 'improving' nature. Loose ballads and folk tales were sung and retailed in home and alehouse. Chapman and hawker peddled 'vulgar and indecent penny books' from door to door, trading on the growing literacy of the common people. There was little popular Christian literature either. The publications of SPCK and Wesley's tracts had only limited sales. Sarah Trimmer's *Instructive Tales* at three shillings a copy were far too expensive for a mass market.

But Tom Paine's *The Rights of Man* (1791), with its call for revolution and the end of monarchy and aristocracy, became a best-seller, which caused alarm and fear among the governing classes. Hannah More had looked at the beginnings of the French Revolution with hope and had welcomed the fall of the Bastille, but, like most English people, was appalled by the increasing terror. She was pressed by her friends, especially Beilby Porteus, to write an antidote to Paine's subversive and irreligious 'poison'. She at first refused, but

As soon as I came to Bath, our dear Bishop of London came to me with a dismal countenance, and told me that I should repent

*it on my death-bed, if I, who knew so much of the habits
and sentiments of the lower order of people, did not write some little
thing tending to open their eyes under their present wild impressions
of liberty and equality . . . In an evil hour, against my will
and my judgment, on one sick day, I scribbled a little pamphlet
called* Village Politics, *by Will Chip; . . . It is as vulgar as heart
can wish; but it is only designed for the most vulgar of
readers. I heartily hope that I shall not be discovered; it is a
sort of writing repugnant to my nature; though indeed it
is rather a question of* peace *than of* politics.[1]

Village Politics (1793) is a dialogue between Jack Anvil, the blacksmith, and Tom Hood, the village mason. Hood wants a new constitution embodying liberty, equality and 'The Rights of Man'. Jack Anvil defends the *status quo* and derides Tom's ideas. Tom's equality would overturn the necessary economic division of labour and make men poorer and not richer. Besides, equality is an illusion since some are stronger and cleverer than others. French liberty is murder; French democracy is government by a thousand tyrants; French equality is pulling down everyone above one; French philosophy is disbelief in God, the devil, heaven and hell; and 'The Rights of Man' are 'battle, murder and sudden death'. It must have pleased Hannah that the villagers of Axbridge burnt an effigy of Tom Paine, but the ensuing celebrations among the men of Axbridge and Shipham in the public houses would not have gained her approval.

When the atheist Dupont, speaking in the French National Assembly, called on the people to overturn the altars of God, Hannah was spurred by the silence of the English bishops to write an open letter in reply. Her *Remarks on the Speech of M. Dupont* called the attention of English people to the horrors of French irreligion. Hannah opened her home in Bath to exiled French priests in England and donated the book's sale proceeds of £240 to their welfare. She was accused by one Protestant pamphlet of being a papist wolf in evangelical clothing and of interfering with the divine will that the French priests should starve.

The success of *Village Politics* convinced Hannah of the tremendous potential for cheap popular literature. She now turned her talents as a writer and organizer to producing pamphlets that she called Cheap Repository Tracts. Her sisters and her Clapham friends lent their assistance and, over the space of three or four years, these tracts turned into a booming cottage industry. Henry Thornton acted as treasurer; Babington and Macaulay were effective agents for the repository; Wilberforce and other wealthy friends were generous subscribers, and Bishop Porteus lent his great influence to the scheme. Between 1795 and 1798, some 114 tracts were published, of which forty-nine can be attributed to Hannah and six to Sally More. Other contributors were Patty More, Henry Thornton, Zachary Macaulay and his wife Selina, John Newton and William Mason.

The tracts consisted of ballads, Sunday readings and stories, some of which were serialized; and they were generally illustrated by lively woodcuts. The tracts, subsidized by subscriptions, sold at a halfpenny, one penny or one penny-halfpenny each — well under the printing and distribution costs. They were printed initially by Samuel Hazard of Bath and then by John Marshall of London, and finally by Evans, Hatchard and Rivington of London. By March 1796, only one year after the commencement of the scheme, over two million copies of the tracts had been distributed, and it is safe to assume that the final sales of the tracts were at least two or three times that number. Distribution was through booksellers, pedlars and hawkers, and friends of the repository. Many copies were bought by the gentry for free distribution. Shiploads were sent overseas, many to America. The tracts were distributed in prisons, schools, hospitals and poorhouses, and among soldiers and sailors.

Five years after Hannah's death, Thompson stated that the tracts formed a principal part of the English cottager's library.[2] Charlotte Yonge estimates that for some twenty years the tracts were a staple fare of such village lending libraries as then existed.[3] But the very success of the tracts led to their demise. The enormous expansion of the whole project overtaxed Hannah's indifferent health, and a tiresome dispute with Marshall, whose interest lay more in profit than the conversion of souls, left her dispirited. She had, however, blazed a trail, which was followed in 1799 by the formation of the Religious Tract Society.

M.G. Jones examines the tracts critically:

Of their kind they rank high. Most of them are vivid, picturesque and dramatic stories, written in simple, forceful and unpretentious English. They are characterised by Miss More's habitual and admirable good sense . . . Character drawing in them is at a minimum.[4]

This is a judgement that Hannah More herself might well have been happy to accept. Her aim was principally to teach religion and morality in homely language. She abandoned any pretence at Johnsonian English in favour of a tongue 'understanded of the people'.

The nature of the tracts is transparent from some of their long titles, for example, *The Story of Sinful Sally. Told by herself. Shewing how from being Sally of the Green she was first led to become Sinful Sally, and afterwards Drunken Sal; and how at last she came to a melancholy, and almost helpless end; being therein a warning to all young women both in town and country*. This tract, which one hastens to add is not attributed to Hannah More, is accompanied by the woodcut of a profligate young woman reclining amid the rubbish on the floor of a ruined barn. In a similar vein is the story of Black Giles the Poacher, containing some account of a family who would rather live by their wits than their work. Giles himself, when engaged in theft, is killed by the fall of a garden wall, but his son, after hearing the eighth commandment, owns up to stealing Widow Brown's apples.

In *The History of Mr Fantom, the new-fashioned Philosopher and Reformist, and his Man William*, Hannah reveals some of the limitations of her individualistic approach to social issues. She has no real concept of corporate responsibility and sees no future in political action to redress social injustices. Injustices must be dealt with on an individual and personal basis. If God allows misery in the world it is that good men may have an opportunity of lessening it. She has an easy time mocking Mr Fantom, a retail trader in the City of London. Fantom seeks to make a name for himself by espousing the new philosophies and radical political theories. He wishes to overthrow all the established order in society.

> *Mr Fantom believed, not in proportion to the strength of the evidence, but to the impudence of the assertion. The trampling on holy ground with dirty shoes, the smearing of the sanctuary with filth and mire, the calling prophets and apostles by the most scurrilous names, the vilifying all established authorities in church and state, was dashing and dazzling. Mr Fantom now being set free from the chains of slavery and superstition, was resolved to show his zeal in the usual way, by trying to free others.*

Fantom seeks to further his campaign for world improvement by converting Mr Trueman, 'an honest, plain and simple-hearted tradesman', whom Fantom despises because 'he paid his taxes without disputing, and read his Bible without doubting'. When he comes to stay, Fantom tells him:

Sir, I have a plan in my head for relieving the miseries of the whole world. Everything is bad as it now stands. I would alter all the laws, and do away with all the religions, and put an end to all the taxes, and all the wars in the world. I would every where redress the injustice of fortune, or what the vulgar call Providence.

Trueman has little time for Fantom's philosophizing. What is needed is more true Christianity. This would do more than all the theorizing to make the world a better place. Trueman is more concerned to deal with practical everyday issues, such as redressing the wrongs suffered by an apprentice cruelly treated by his master, or rescuing a fellow tradesman from the debtors' gaol. Fantom, however, is too mean to contribute a single guinea to help set this man free. Hannah expresses her contempt for such an attitude by having Trueman say:

Well, Mr Fantom, you are a wonderful man to keep up such a stock of benevolence at so small an expense. To love mankind so dearly, and yet avoid all opportunities of doing good; to have such a noble zeal for the millions, and to feel so little compassion for the units; surely none but a philosopher could indulge so much philanthropy, and so much frugality at the same time.

The story has a melodramatic ending. Fantom's servant, William, runs off with his master's port and his mistress's silver spoons. He is next heard of in Chelmsford Prison, lying under sentence of death for murder. Trueman persuades Fantom to accompany him to visit William in prison. In prison William accuses Fantom of making him a drunkard, a thief and a murderer, by denying the reality of future judgment. Fantom sneaks off home but Trueman spends the night with the condemned man reading the Gospel to him and urging his repentance.

Other tracts give a vivid glimpse into the social history of the times gleaned from the sisters' visits to the homes of the Mendip villagers. In *The Shepherd of Salisbury Plain*, 'a story from real life', Hannah portrays an honest labourer struggling to bring up a family of eight children on eight shillings a week. The children begin to earn money when as young as five years old. The girls receive a halfpenny a day, and later a penny a day, by knitting, and the boys make similar sums by scare-crowing or stone-picking in the fields. Little Molly gathers the wool left by the sheep on brambles in the hills, and her poor mother, crippled by rheumatism, cards this wool into shape. The biggest girl spins the wool into thread, which the children knit into stockings for themselves. The father mends the children's shoes for the umpteenth time, because his self-respect will not allow them to run around barefoot. The family lives in a hovel with one room above and one below. They hardly ever have a fire and they seldom cook. Sunday dinner is a large dish of potatoes, a piece of coarse bread and a brown pitcher of water. The scanty furniture in the cottage consists of a table, four brown wooden chairs, an old carved elbow chair and a chest with a candlestick. By the tiny grate there is an iron pot and kettle and a bright spit, which is kept for ornament and not for use. The handful of coal in the grate is taken out as soon as the kettle boils.

Turn the Carpet, a philosophical conversation between two carpet weavers, is judged by Charlotte Yonge the best of Hannah's tracts. Bishop Porteus after reading it commented, 'There you have Bishop Butler's Analogy all for a half-penny.' The story, written as a ballad, hinges on the fact that a carpet pattern is woven on its reverse side. Hannah draws the moral that life too takes place on the reverse side of God's providential ordering of the world, and that life's mysteries will be understood only when we see the whole pattern in the light of eternity.

> *This world which clouds thy soul with doubt*
> *Is but a carpet inside out;*
> *As when we view these shreds and ends,*
> *We know not what the whole intends;*
> *So when on earth things look but odd;*
> *They're working out some scheme of God.*
> *What now seem random strokes will there*
> *In order and design appear.*
> *Then we shall praise what here we spurn'd,*
> *For then the carpet shall be turn'd.*

The political nature of some of the tracts invited the criticism that Hannah had written the tracts at the request of the Government, even of the Prime Minister, Pitt himself. But there is no substance to this. The tracts were the instinctive response of a religious and patriotic woman to what she considered the needs of the times. Her political conservatism was in no way self-interested or based on an ignorance of the poverty of the rural poor. Rather it arose from the deeply held conviction that constitutional and social upheaval would aggravate and not redress the situation. About twenty years later Hannah More did, however, make one last foray into the world of popular journalism, and this time in response to a direct invitation from the government of the day. She told Sir William Pepys:

> *I did not think to turn ballad-monger in my old age. But the strong and urgent representations I have had from the highest quarters of the very alarming temper of the times, and the spirit of revolution which shews itself more or less in all the manufacturing towns, has led me to undertake as a duty a task I should gladly have avoided. I have written many songs, papers, &c by way of antidote to this fatal poison. Thousands and tens of thousands have been circulated without it being known from what source they proceeded.*[5]

The year 1817 was a time of bread riots, machine breaking and rick burning. Much of the discord was fomented by the radical *Cobbett's Weekly Political Register* and its cheap popular version, the *Twopenny Register*, which Hannah regarded as blasphemous and seditious. In reply, she contributed articles to the *Anti-Cobbett*, or *Weekly Patriotic Register*, a penny-halfpenny journal intended by the authorities to answer Cobbett's radicalism. The *Anti-Cobbett* was short-lived; it ceased publication when Cobbett fled the country after the suspension of the *Habeas Corpus* Act. The Mendip peasantry remained loyal throughout this period and Hannah must have drawn great pleasure from the loyal address signed by every Shipham man expressing disapproval of the riots and agitation in 1819.

Extravagant claims were made for the impact of Miss More's tracts. It was alleged that in 1796, a year of scarcity, the singing of her ballad *The Riot*, or *Half a Loaf is Better than No Bread* effectively checked 'a very formidable riot' in Bath. Again it was said that *Patient Joe* or *The Newcastle Collier* had solved all the industrial problems of the north of England. But a more sober opinion was that of the educationalist, J.C. Colquhoun, who, writing some thirty years after Hannah's death, quoted with approval the widely held opinion that the great improvement in religion and morals since the beginning of Victoria's reign was due to Robert Raikes' Sunday schools and Hannah More's writings.[6] Cobbett's attack on Hannah for uniting the cause of religion with the defence of the established order was an unwitting tribute to her effectiveness as a propagandist.

Modern scholars have also noted the extraordinary transformation which took place over this period in the sphere of domestic life and personal ethics. D.H. Newsome calls the evangelicals the fathers of the Victorians.[7] Professor Harold Perkin has written:

> *Between 1780 and 1850 the English ceased to be one of the most aggressive, brutal, rowdy, outspoken, riotous, cruel and bloodthirsty nations in the world and became one of the most inhibited, polite, orderly, tender-minded, prudish and hypocritical.*[8]

15
THE SPIRITUAL WRITER

It is impossible to pray sincerely
for the well-being of others, without being
desirous of contributing to it.

The Spirit of Prayer

Devotional writings are creations of their own age and rarely appeal to future generations. The writings of Hannah More are no exception. They are not read today. But yet, when we blow the dust off these ancient leather-bound volumes, we can begin to understand why Hannah's writings were so popular in their own day. They are beautifully written by a practised author, and combine a lively turn of phrase with deep human and spiritual insight. Maybe we too shall find in them some lessons for our own generation.

Hannah was aware that to set oneself up as a moral or spiritual writer is a risky business. There is the danger of hypocrisy. Hannah knew that it is much easier to preach than to practise. She wrestled with this in her own life. Her critics could know nothing of her inner struggle of soul. (Hannah, by the way, always referred to herself as a writer in the masculine.)

> *The triumphant detector of the discordance between the author and his book knows not the secret regrets, hears not the fervent prayers, witnesses not the penitential sorrows, which a deep sense of this disagreement produces in the self-abasing heart.*[1]

There is the danger of pretentiousness. Hannah liked to tell of the earnest Welsh minister who proposed to publish a sermon.

He consulted Hannah over how many thousand copies he should have printed. Hannah persuaded him to reduce from thousands to hundreds, not daring to suggest scores. In the event only half a dozen copies were sold, bought by the charity of his friends. Yet this same minister sought out Hannah on her return from London and seriously enquired whether she had noticed any material improvement in London life since the publication of his sermon.

There is also the risk of being ridiculed and laughed at by the cynical. To the wit who scoffed, 'To mend the world's a vast design,' Hannah countered:

> *It is indeed, a design, from which the purity of his motive may not always secure the humility of the author. Yet modestly to aim at ameliorating that little portion of it which lies within his immediate sphere, is a duty out of which he should not be laughed by wits and epigrammists. Instead of indulging unfounded hopes of improbable effects, the Christian writer will be humbled at the mortifying reflection, what great and extensive evil the most insignificant bad man may effect, while so little comparative good may be accomplished by the best.[2]*

Hannah's writings breathe a deep conviction that Christianity irradiates the whole business of life and has universal significance and importance:

> *The truly catholic spirit of Christianity accommodates itself . . . to the circumstances of the whole human race. It rejects none on account of their pecuniary wants, their personal infirmities, or their intellectual deficiencies. [The goodness of God has appointed] one wide, comprehensive, and universal means of salvation: a salvation, of which all are invited to partake; by a means which all are capable of using; which nothing but voluntary blindness can prevent our comprehending, and nothing but wilful error can hinder us from embracing.[3]*

To Hannah religion was too important to be left to old age. To those who argued that they would consider the claims of religion when they were tired of life and had nothing better to do, she replied:

> *Do they not forget, that to perform this great business well requires all the strength of their youth, and all the vigour of their*

unimpaired capacities? . . . Let them reflect how little able they
will be to transact the most important of all business, in the moment
of excruciating pain, or in the day of universal debility . . . To put
off religion till we have lost all taste for amusement . . . and
not to devote our days to heaven till we have 'no pleasure in them'
ourselves, is but an ungracious offering. And it is a wretched
sacrifice to the God of Heaven, to present him with the remnants of
decayed appetites, and the leavings of extinguished passions.[4]

So far as Hannah was concerned, Christianity meant biblical religion. She believed that there was as much difference between reading the Bible mechanically and reading it spiritually as there was between pouring a fluid on the ground and distilling it drop by drop. She advised therefore that the reading of scripture be approached with the following attitude:

This book is not a work of fancy. I do not therefore read it
for amusement, but instruction; but am I seriously proposing to read
it like one who has a deep interest in its contents? Is it my sincere
intention to convert the knowledge I am about to acquire into
any practical application in my own case? Is it my earnest wish to
improve the state of my own heart by comparing it with what
I allow to be the only perfect rule of faith and practice?[5]

She summarized the Bible's teaching with masterful succinctness when giving her advice about the education of Princess Charlotte:

The great leading truths of Scripture are few in number, though
the spirit of them is diffused through every page. — The being
and attributes of the Almighty; the spiritual worship which he
requires; the introduction of natural and moral evil into the world;
the restoration of man; the life, death, character and offices of
the Redeemer; the holy example he has given us; the divine system
of ethics which he has bequeathed us; the awful sanctions with
which they are enforced; the spiritual nature of the eternal world;
the necessity of repentance; the pardon of sin through faith in
a Redeemer; the offer of divine assistance; and the promise of
eternal life.[6]

Such scriptural principles need to be taught from an early age so that they form habits for life:

*To implant these dispositions, then, is the leading object of what we
may venture to call the Scripture philosophy. And as the heart must
be the seat of that which is to influence the whole man, so
it is chiefly to the heart that the holy Scriptures address themselves.
Their object is to make us* love *what is* right, *rather than to
occupy our understandings with its theory.* Knowledge puffeth
up, *says one of our divine instructors,* but it is Love that
edifieth. *And the principle which is here affirmed, will be
found most strictly true, that if a love of goodness be once
thoroughly implanted, we shall not need many rules; but
we shall act aright from what we may almost call a noble kind
of instinct.*[7]

How then are Christians to conduct themselves in the world?
Hannah had little doubt that our true destiny is to be found in
hard work and the proper use of time. Therein lies the secret of
real happiness.

*We were not sent into this world with orders to make ourselves
miserable, but with abilities, and directions, and helps, to search
out the best possibilities of happiness which remain to beings,
fallen from that state of moral and mental rectitude in which
man was created . . . Human life, therefore, abounding as it
does in blessings and mercies, is not the blissful vision which
youthful fancy images, or poetry feigns, or romance exhibits. It is
in considerable measure compounded of painful and dull realities,
and not a splendid tissue of grand events or brilliant exploits;
it is to some an almost unvaried state of penury, to many a
series of cares and troubles, to all, a state of probation . . . And
whether we consider the manual industry of the poor, or the
intellectual exertions of the superior classes, we shall find that
diligent occupation, if not criminally perverted from its purposes, is
at once the instrument of virtue and the secret of happiness.
Man cannot be safely trusted with a life of leisure.*[8]

Here lies the spirit of the coming age of Victoria, an age which
purported to turn its back on the self-indulgence of the Regency
period and to find its purpose in the manifold duties of religion
and industry.

Hannah taught that Christians in the world were to make neither
a parade nor a secret of their religion. They were to perform all
sorts of kindnesses with cheerfulness. They were to use their

time and their wealth, not for luxury and dissipation, but for the good of others, while avoiding a frugal or miserly spirit. *Candidus* is the name that Hannah gives her ideal Christian. He is described as a good lover, but a bad hater. He is a man of moderation and wise judgment. 'He has learned from the errors of two opposite parties, that fanaticism teaches men to despise religion and bigotry to hate it.'[9] Although truly attached to the worship and doctrine of the Church of England, *Candidus* is not a party man and is ready to recognize a genuine Christian in those who wear a different denominational label. He is distinguished by consistency of conduct.

> *The confirmed Christian exemplifies the emphatical description of the good man in Scripture, 'he walks with God'. He does not approach him at stated times; he does not ceremoniously address him on great occasions only, and then retreat, and dwell at a distance; but he walks with him, his habitual intercourse, his natural motion, his daily converse, his intimate communication, is with his Redeemer: and he remembers that walking not only implies intercourse, but progress . . . The nearer he approaches to God, the more in one sense he will be sensible of his distance from him . . . Yet this growing consciousness only serves to augment his love.[10]*

Hannah was impatient with the nominal Christianity which was very much the spirit of her age. She described the nominal Christian in a memorable phrase as 'the decorous sensualist' and portrayed him with devastating insight:

> *[His] life is a course of sober luxury, of measured indulgence. He contrives to reconcile an abandonment of sound principle with a kind of orderly practice. He enquires rather what is decent than what is right; what will require the favourable opinion of the world, especially his own class, rather than what will please God. His object is to make the most of this world. Selfishness has established its throne in his heart. His study is to make every thing and every person subservient to his own convenience, or pleasure, or profit, yet without glaringly trespassing on the laws of propriety or custom. — Self is the source and centre of all his actions; but though this governing principle is always on the watch for its gratification, yet, as part of that gratification depends on a certain degree of reputation, it frequently leads him to do the*

right things, though without right motives . . . He goes to church
on all public occasions, but without devotion; gives alms without
charity; subscribes to public institutions without being interested in
their prosperity, except as they are frequently succeeded by a
pleasant dinner and good company, and as the subsription-list of
names he knows will be published . . . He never does a small
kindness without a view to asking a greater . . . Prayer never
enters into his plans, — for he has nothing to ask, for he has all in
himself, — thanksgiving is still less his practice; for what he has he
deserves . . . But as to the laws of God he thinks they were made
to guard the possessions of the rich, to punish the wicked poor,
and to frighten those who have nothing to lose. Yet he respects some
of the commandments and would placard on every post and pillar
that which says, 'Thou shalt not steal'; whilst he thinks that
which says, 'Thou shalt not covet', might be expunged from the
Decalogue.[11]

There is in this passage a rare radicalism which enables us to
recognize that the decorous sensualist is still alive and well at
the end of the twentieth century. Closely related to the decorous
sensualists are the 'Borderers', which was the name that Hannah
gave to the fence-sitters who try to accommodate themselves to
both the world and religion, seeking to keep on good terms with
both.

Their chief difficulty arises when they happen to meet the
inhabitants of both territories together; yet so ingenious are they in
the art of trimming, that they contrive not to lose much ground with
either. When alone with one party, they take care never
to speak warmly of the absent. With the worldly they smile, and
perhaps good-naturedly shake their head at some little scruples, and
some excess of strictness in the absent party . . . With the religious
colony, they tenderly lament the necessity imposed upon them
of being obliged to associate so much with neighbours from whom,
they confess, there is not much to be learned, while they
own there is something to be feared.[12]

If these things seem trivial Hannah needed to remind her readers
that nominal Christianity posed a threat to the real thing. This kind
of temporizing is 'not saving Christianity. It is not that spiritual,
yet practical religion, for which the Son of God endured the cross,
that he might establish it in the hearts of his followers.'[13] Eternal

issues were at stake. 'If we come short of heaven, whether we lose it by more or fewer steps, the failure is equally decisive, the loss equally irreparable.'[14] There could be no cheap salvation. Mental assent to the truths of Christianity was no substitute for obedience. It was a deception 'to suppose that we shall possess hereafter what we do not desire here, that we shall complete then, what we do not think of beginning now'.[15]

> Do not, then, any longer make religion an incidental item in
> your scheme of life. Do not turn over the consideration of it
> to chance; make it a part of your daily plan; take it up as a set
> business; give it an allotted portion in the distribution of your daily
> concerns, while you admit it as the pervading principle of them
> all. You carry on no other transaction casually; you do not conduct
> your profession or manage your estate by fits and starts. You
> do not expect your secular business to go on well without minding
> it. You set about it intently; you transact it with a fixed design; you
> consider it as a definite object. You would not be satisfied with
> it, if it brought you no return, still less would you be satisfied not to
> know whether it brought any return or not. Yet you are contented as
> to this great business of life, though you perceive no evidence
> of its progress. You see no absurdity in a religious profession which
> leaves you as indigent as it found you. Does it not look as if your
> sincerity, in the one case, did not keep pace with your earnestness in
> the other; as if your religion was a shadow, and your secular
> concerns were the only reality?[16]

Eighteenth-century England professed to be Christian, but by and large it embraced only a nominal religion. Fashionable people tended to regard religion as something venerable like the law of the land, 'a valuable institution for the preservation of the public good; but it does not interest their feelings'.[17] Such people attended church and observed the outward trappings of religion, but scorned any demonstration of enthusiasm. Hannah was intolerant of such nominalism which she saw as undermining the very faith it professed to uphold.

> A theology which depresses the standards, which overlooks the
> motives, which dilutes the doctrines, softens the precepts, lowers the
> sanctions, and mutilates the scheme of Christianity; which merges it
> in undefined generalities, which makes it consist in a system of
> morals which might be interwoven into almost any religion; . . . a

theology which neither makes Jesus Christ the foundation, nor
the Holy Spirit the efficient agent, nor inward renovation a leading
principle, nor humility a distinguishing characteristic; which
insists on a good heart, but demands not a renewed heart; which
inserts virtues into the stock of the old nature, but insists
not on the necessity of a changed nature; — such a theology is not
that which the costly apparatus of Christianity was designed
to present to us.[18]

Hannah was a great believer in the need to form good habits.
Habits could be used for good or bad purposes, to offend or please
our Maker. The value of habits is that

the right principle which first set them at work continues to keep
them at it, and finally becomes so prevalent, that there is a kind of
spontaneity in the act, which keeps up the energy, without constant
reference to the spring which first set it in motion. Good habits are
good dispositions ripened by repetition into virtue, and sanctified
by prayer into holiness.[19]

Bad habits are not easily abandoned. Hannah cites the example of
the love of money. The new convert is persuaded that there is no
such thing as a Christian without generosity.

The profession is cheap, the practice is costly. An occasion
is brought home to him, of exercising the grace he has been
commending. He acknowledges its force, he does more, he feels it.
If taken at the moment, something considerable might be done;
but if any delay intervene, that delay is fatal; for from feeling, he
begins to calculate. Now there is a cooling property in calculation,
which freezes the warm current that sensibility had set in
motion. The old habit is too powerful for the young convert, yet he
flatters himself that he has at once exercised charity and
discretion. He takes comfort both from the liberal feeling which had
resolved to give the money, and the prudence which had
saved it, laying to his heart the flattering unction, that he has only
spared it for some more pressing demand, which, when it occurs,
will again set him on feeling, and calculating, and saving.[20]

How well she knew the human heart, her own and her reader's!
How well Hannah knew too that we fritter away time and
opportunity by submitting to what she called the 'uncontrolled
dominion of a roving imagination':

*This prolific faculty produces such a constant budding of images,
fancies, visions, conjectures and conceits, that she can subsist
plentifully on her own independent stock. She is perpetually
wandering from the point to which she promised to confine herself
when she set out; is ever roaming from the spot to which
her powerless possessor had threatened to pin her down. We retire
with a resolution to reflect: Reason has no sooner marshalled
her forces than this undisciplined run-away escapes from duty, one
straggler after another joins the enemy, or brings home some
foreign impertinence. While we meant to indulge only a harmless
reflection, we are brought under subjection to a whole series
of reveries of different characters and opposite descriptions. Fresh
trains obliterate our first speculations, till the spirit sinks into a sort
of deliquium. We have nothing for it but resolutely to resist
the enfeebling despot. Let us stir up some counteracting force: let us
fly to some active employment which will break the charm,
and dissolve the thraldom. No matter what, so it be innocent and
opposite. We shall not cure ourselves by the sturdiest resolution not
to do this thing which is complained of, unless we compel
ourselves to do something else. Courageous exertion is the only
conqueror of irresolution: vigorous action the only supplanter of idle
speculation.*[21]

Here Hannah offers us a key to much in her own life. Her way
to deal with romantic day-dreams or disappointed hopes was to
throw herself into a frenzy of activity and work. Every Christian,
she believed, is called upon to exercise charity, which she describes
as an energy that empowers every other virtue, and that stems
from the love of Christ himself. Charity, for Hannah, was not
sentimental but essentially practical. She quoted with approval
Lord Bacon's remark that 'riches, when kept in a heap, are
corrupt like a dunghill, but when spread abroad, diffuse beauty
and fertility'.

*[Love] is not a solitary virtue, but is inseparably linked with truth
and equity . . . She leads us perpetually to examine our means,
dispositions and opportunities, and exert their combined force for
the promotion of the greatest possible good . . . We must not
judge of our charity by single acts and particular instances, but by
our general tendencies and propensities. We must strive after a
uniformity in our charity . . . If we are unkind and illiberal in one*

*instance as we are profuse in another, when the demand is equal,
and we have both the choice and the means, whatever we may
be, we are not charitable.*[22]

Here we see that principle of consistency which was so strong a
trait in Hannah's life and writings. She believed that everything
which we possess is held in trust for God and that one day he will
call us to account for the use of whatever talents he has given to us.
The greater our gifts and abilities the more will be expected of us.
But none can escape the day of reckoning:

> *Do not many of us, like him we are so ready to condemn, conceal
> our self-love under the assumption of modesty, and indulge our
> sloth under the humble pretence that we have no talent to exercise?
> But let us be assured it is the deadness of our spiritual affections,
> and not our mean opinion of ourselves, that is the real cause.
> The service of God is irksome, because his commands interfere with
> our self-indulgence.*[23]

Time was a particular talent prone to abuse. Hannah herself seems
to have been a particularly good manager of this limited resource.

> *He who carefully governs his mind will conscientiously regulate his
> time. To him who thus accurately distributes it, who appropriates
> the hour to its due employment, life will never seem tedious,
> yet counted by this moral arithmetic it will be really long. If we
> compute our time as critically as our other possessions; if we
> assign its proportions to its duties, though the divisions will then be
> so fully occupied that they will never drag, yet the aggregate
> sum will be found sufficiently long for all the purposes to which life
> is destined.*[24]

So it is necessary that we make proper plans for the use of our time,
but we must not be blindly inflexible.

> *Both ourselves and our plans must be ever kept subject to the
> will of a higher power. That is an ill-regulated mind which wears
> life away without any settled scheme of action; that is a little
> mind which makes itself a slave to any preconceived rule, when a
> more imperative duty may arise to demand its infraction.*[25]

Of all the uses to which we may put our time, none is more
important than prayer. It is necessary to choose set times for
prayer.

*That which is turned over to any chance-time is seldom done at
all . . . Other duties and engagements have their allotted seasons;
why, then, should the most important duty in which an immortal
being can be employed, by being left to accident, become liable to
occasional omission, liable to increasing neglect, liable to total
oblivion? . . . [But they] who most insist on the value of stated
devotions, must never lose sight of that grand, and universal
prime truth, that wherever we are, we are still in God's presence;
whatever we have is his gift; whatever we hope is his promise.[26]*

Why then does God not always seem to answer our prayers? This
is a mystery.

*Infinite Wisdom is not obliged to inform us of the manner,
or the time, of his operations; what he expects of us is to persevere
in the duty. The very obedience to the command is no small
thing, whatever be its imperceptible effects . . . He neither grants
nor denies any thing which is not accurately weighed and
measured; which is not exactly suited to their wants, if not to their
requests . . . In prayer we must take care not to measure
our necessities by our desires; the former are few, the latter may be
insatiable.[27]*

Prayer promotes true contentment and patience. True contentment
is always praising God for what she possesses. True patience is
ready to suffer the loss of what she has. The language of patience
is the language of Job, 'Shall I not receive evil from the hand of
the Lord as well as good?' The loss of true peace of mind in prayer
may be the result of some secret sin, some evil imagination, some
secretly cherished corruption in the mind.

*Not being accustomed to control at other times, it intrudes when
you would willingly expel it; for a guest which is unreservedly let in
at other seasons, and cordially entertained, will too frequently
break in when you desire to be alone . . . To the close bosom sin,
knowing that no human charge can be brought against it, the soul
habitually returns with a fondness facilitated by long indulgence,
and only whetted by a short separation.[28]*

Hannah More lived and died in the sure confidence of God's
control over his world and over her destiny. God's providence was
the source of her hope, the reason for her persistence:

129

It is not easy to conceive a more deplorable state of mind, than
to live in a disbelief of God's providential ordering of the world.
To be threatened with troubles, and see no power which can avert
them; to be surrounded with sorrows, and discern no hand which
can redress them; to labour under oppression or calumny, and
believe there is no friend to relieve, and no judge to vindicate us; to
live in a world, of which we believe its Ruler has abdicated
the throne, or delegated its direction to chance; to suspect that he
has made over the triumph to injustice, and the victory to impiety;
to suppose that we are abandoned to the casualties of nature,
and the domination of wickedness; to behold the earth a scene of
disorder, with no superintendent to regulate it; to hear the storms
beating, and see the tempests spreading desolation around, with no
influence to direct, and no wisdom to control them: all this would
render human life a burden intolerable to human feeling. Even a
heathen, in one of those glimpses of illumination which they seemed
occasionally to catch, could say, it would not be worth while
to live in a world which was not governed by Providence.[29]

Hannah's Christianity was never an escapist religion, a mere closet
pietism. Her religion was essentially practical and one to be lived
out in the world.

Until, then, we make our religion a part of our common life,
until we bring Christianity . . . from its retreat to live in the world,
and dwell among men; until we have brought it from the closet to
the active scene, from the church to the world, whether that world
be the court, the senate, the exchange, the public office, the private
counting-house, the courts of justice, the professional departments,
or the domestic drawing-room, it will not have fully accomplished
what it was sent on earth to do.[30]

We must leave Hannah's writings as she bares something of her
own private struggle of soul:

When those with whom he occasionally mixes sees the praying
Christian calm and cheerful in society, they little suspect the
frequent struggles, the secret conflicts, he has within. Others see his
devout and conscientious life, but he alone knows the plague of
his own heart. If he has a conflict within the world he has a harder
conflict with sin. His bosom foe is his most unyielding enemy. This,

130

therefore, is that which makes his other trials heavy, which makes his power of sustaining them weak, which renders his conquest over them slow and inconclusive; which too often solicits him to oppose interest to duty, indolence to resistance, and self-indulgence to victory.[31]

16
THE HONOURED PHILANTHROPIST

The hour of prayer or meditation
is a consecration of the hours employed . . .
In those hours we may lay in a stock of grace,
which if faithfully improved,
will shed its odour on every portion of the day.

Christian Morals

In 1801 Hannah, having sold Cowslip Green, and the sisters, having disposed of the house in Bath, moved to a comfortable new residence which they had had built at Barley Wood in Wrington Parish. Wrington, then a village with 163 houses and about 850 inhabitants, was the birthplace of the philosopher, John Locke (1632-1704). The new house at Barley Wood was begun in 1800 but suffered delays and the death of the first builder. It was a two-storey house built of stone, with a thatched roof. A rustic verandah ran round the ground floor and this was soon draped with jasmine, honeysuckle, roses, woodbine and clematis. From the front verandah Hannah could look south at the long line of the Mendip Hills. The landscape was described by the author Thomas De Quincey, whose mother had a villa at Wrington, as a beautiful series of rolling downs, like vast lawns eaten close by sheep, on which one could roam on horseback for miles. The house at Barley Wood was for many years in the possession of the Wills family, and was until recently the head office of a large industrial organization. It has now been acquired by a trust which seeks to help people to recover from the effects of alcohol and drug addiction. One senses that Hannah More would approve.

The More sisters desired to spend their remaining days in the care of the poor, in reading and in reflection. Hannah, however, enjoyed little leisure. She would say that her only claim to fame was to have written eleven books after the age of sixty. As late as 1819, when well, she still devoted some five hours each morning to writing. She had made substantial earnings from her writings and confessed to having made £30,000 from her books. Mrs Hall later reported that Hannah More gave some £900 a year to charity.

The Mores were now established in the good esteem of the neighbouring nobility and gentry. Their local visitors included Lady Waldegrave and her mother, the Duchess of Gloucester; Hiley Addington, MP, of Langford Court; the Hart-Davises and the De Quinceys. Dr and Mrs Whalley of Mendip Lodge brought the famous actress, Mrs Siddons and the poet Anna Seward, known as 'the Swan of Lichfield'. Anna thought Hannah too pious. Hannah thought Anna too sentimental.

Another regular visitor was John Harford of Blaise Castle. Harford is believed to be the model on which Hannah based her hero in her only novel, *Coelebs*. He has left us a thumbnail sketch of the sisters in 1809, who 'in their style of dress and manners belong to a society far away'. Mary, grave, dignified and rather deaf, was the acknowledged head of the household. Betty good-natured and hospitable managed the household affairs. Sally, with her sparkling sense of humour, was the wit and the flower arranger of the family. Patty, the youngest of the family with bright blue eyes and smiling face, was the untiring activist and doer of good works. Hannah wore an elaborate white muslin hat and a white fichu, or triangular shawl, for the shoulders. Hannah, whose 'brilliant eyes lit up a pale but sensible countenance, was most frank and cordial. There was no effort to shine, but again and again pointed and bright things fell from her lips in the most easy and natural manner'.[1]

Hannah and Patty were the storm-troopers of the sisters' philanthropy. They visited the houses of the poor, made garments for the children, assisted the women's clubs and maintained the three Greater Schools at Cheddar, Shipham and Nailsea on 'a peace footing'. Every Sunday from May to December, except when rising waters made travelling impossible, the sisters would visit one or other of their Sunday schools. When they had guests they used a farm wagon as transport. At other times they walked or rode on horseback behind Charles the groom.

In a letter dated 1801, Hannah told Wilberforce of her teaching methods in the Sunday schools. She would open in the morning with Sunday school prayers from the *Cheap Repository Tracts*. The school was divided into a Bible class, a Testament class and a psalter class. Those who could not read at all were questioned out of *The Questions for the Mendip Schools* and the *Church Catechism*, which Hannah had herself devised. When teaching the Testament or Bible class, Hannah always began with the parables, especially those in chapter 15 of Luke's Gospel — 'The Lost Sheep', 'The Lost Coin' and 'The Lost Son' — which she explained so that the pupils understood their sense and their practical application. She then spent time with the first three chapters of the book of Genesis, so that the doctrine of the fall was firmly grasped. She used small bribes of a penny a chapter so that the children would learn by heart certain fundamental passages of Scripture, particularly chapters 9 and 53 of the book of Isaiah, Psalm 51, the Sermon on the Mount in chapter 5 of Matthew's Gospel, and parts of Jesus' discourses in John's Gospel. School finished for the little ones at five o'clock with a hymn and a prayer. But the older children and their parents were invited to come back to the school at six when someone would read a short sermon to them. Hannah specially commended Burder's *Village Sermons*.

The children received frequent rewards. They got one penny for attending four Sundays in a row. Each year prizes for merit consisted of a Bible, a Prayer Book or a *Cheap Repository Tract*. Once in six or eight weeks Hannah would distribute a little gingerbread. Annually the boys received a hat, a shirt, or shoes, according to their wants; the big girls a calico apron and cap; and the little girls, a cap and a tippet of calico — a cotton cape or muffler which covers the shoulders and the upper body.

> *It is my grand endeavour to make every thing as entertaining*
> *as I can, and to try and engage their affections; to excite in*
> *them the love of God; and particularly to awaken their gratitude to*
> *their Redeemer. When they seem to get a little tired, we change*
> *the scene; and by standing up, and singing a hymn, their attention*
> *is relieved. I have never tried the system of terror, because I*
> *have found that kindness produces a better end by better means.*[2]

This is a far cry from the popular caricature of the Victorian teacher and shows that Hannah was in many respects years ahead of her time in her understanding of children and in her enlightened approach to classroom teaching.

In her book *The Spirit of Prayer*, published in 1825, Hannah set out a scheme of prayer for young persons modelled on the

Lord's Prayer from Matthew's Gospel, chapter 6. She believed that mothers should teach their children the Lord's Prayer, taking one sentence or clause at a time and explaining its meaning.

> *All explanations should be made in the most plain and familiar*
> *terms, it being words, and not things, which commonly perplex*
> *children, if, as it sometimes happens, the teacher, though not*
> *wanting sense, wants perspicuity and simplicity . . . I would have*
> *it understood, that by these little comments I do not mean that*
> *children should be put to learn dry, and to them, unintelligible*
> *expositions: but that the exposition is to be colloquial . . . If*
> *they are made to commit [written forms of prayer] to memory like a*
> *couple of verses, and to repeat them in a dry customary way, they*
> *will produce little effect on their minds. They will not understand*
> *what they repeat, if we do not early open to them the important*
> *scheme* of prayer.[3]

The growing strength of evangelicalism within and without the Church of England led to a great flowering of missionary and voluntary societies at the turn of the eighteenth century. The sisters gave these societies their active support. Hannah took a personal interest in the affairs of the newly fledged Church Missionary Society. In 1826, after the missionary meeting in Bristol, 'three carriages full of holy missionaries and missionesses'[4] paid court to her in her eighty-second year. Hannah established a branch of the inter-denominational British and Foreign Bible Society in Wrington Parish. The first annual meeting of the branch was held in 1816. Hannah was overjoyed with the response.

> *We had near forty clergymen of the Establishment, so that even*
> *Archdeacon — cannot plant us in his 'hot bed of heresy and*
> *schism.' When the meeting was over, which was held in the*
> *waggon-yard, as there was no room for them in the inn, all*
> *the superior part of the company resorted, by previous invitation, to*
> *Barley Wood. A hundred and one sat down to dinner, and about*
> *one hundred and sixty to tea. Happily it was a fine day, and*
> *above fifty dined under the trees, — the overflowings from our*
> *small house. They all enjoyed themselves exceedingly, and it had*
> *all the gaiety of a public garden.*[5]

The stream of visitors was unending. Barley Wood became a place of pilgrimage for bishops and ecclesiastics visiting Bristol.

Alexander Knox, a layman who visited from Dublin, called Barley Wood 'a minor evangelical centre' for the number of clergy who passed through its doors; men like Henry Ryder (the first evangelical churchman of his generation to be made a bishop, first of Gloucester, then Lichfield), Daniel Wilson (who became Bishop of Calcutta and transformed the Anglican church in India), Rowland Hill (the popular preacher who built Surrey Chapel in Blackfriars), Edward Bickersteth (the founder of a long line of evangelical Anglican clergy) and Thomas Biddulph (the Rector of St James, Bristol, where the More sisters worshipped for many years). Dr Richard Beadon, Bishop of Bath and Wells, although not an evangelical, was a warm supporter and frequent visitor. Successive Bishops of Bristol, Dr Mansel and Dr Grey, visited Hannah, and John Jebb, Bishop of Limerick, came to see her from Ireland. 'There is,' wrote Jebb, 'no modern author, whom I hold in such estimation; indeed veneration . . . would more adequately express my feelings.'[6]

The nobility, Americans, poets — all came to pay their respects. Joseph Cottle, the Bristol publisher, brought Samuel Taylor Coleridge to Barley Wood in 1814. Coleridge was offended when, after talking to him for two hours, Hannah deserted him for a titled lady, leaving the poet with the sisters. But Wordsworth, according to the antagonistic de Quincey, 'made a conquest of holy Hannah'.[7] There were also regular visits from Hannah's Clapham friends. A charming description of such a visit comes from Henry Thornton's daughter, Marianne, writing in 1856:

I have this year visited the paradise of my childhood and fancied I could once more see the venerable forms and hear the kind greetings of the hospitable sisters. Surely there was never a house so full of intellect and piety and active benevolence. They live in such uninterrupted harmony with each other; were so full of their separate pursuits, enjoyed with such intense vivacity all the pleasures of their beautiful home, so wholly laid aside the forms of society that were irksome, that young and old felt in a brighter and happier world . . . I can imagine our arrival and 'the ladies' as they were always called, rushing out to cover us with kisses and take us to the kitchen, to exhibit us to Mary and Charles, the housemaid and coachman, then running to fetch the tea-things, Mrs. Betty letting no-one but herself fry the bacon and eggs for the darlings.

Marianne goes on to tell of the loaves of mahogany colour and enormous size, baked only once a week; of the two cats called 'Passive Obedience' and 'Non-resistance' who 'were fed by us all day long'; of the crowns of flowers the children made for themselves and the garlands for the sheep; and, when they had laid themselves down on the hay to rest, 'Charles the coachman, gardener, bailiff and carpenter made us a syllabub [a dish of frothy or curdled cream] under the cow.'[8]

One specially welcome guest was the young son of Zachary and Selina Macaulay, Thomas Babington Macaulay, the future historian. According to Sir George Trevelyan, Hannah More was 'the most affectionate and wisest of friends, and readily undertook the superintendence of his studies, his pleasures and his health. She would keep him with her for weeks.'[9] Hannah told his parents of Tom's stay and of his passion for writing verses: 'We have poetry for breakfast, dinner and supper.'[10] When Tom was six she wrote him a delightful letter, enclosing some money for books:

> Though you are a little boy now, you will one day, if it please God, be a man; but before you are a man, I hope that you will be a scholar. I therefore wish you to purchase such books as will be useful and agreeable to you then . . . Employ this very small sum in laying a little corner-stone for your future library.[11]

The Macaulays consulted Hannah on Tom's education. She showed a strong evangelical dislike of public schools (independent schools, mainly boarding) which, with their almost complete absence of religious education, she regarded as 'nurseries of vice'. Hannah shared great pride in Tom's academic successes. Unhappily at the end of her life she parted company from him on the issue of parliamentary reform, and she revoked a valuable bequest of books from her library in his favour. But Thomas Macaulay bore Hannah no ill will. Many years later he visited Barley Wood with the sisters' old friend, John Harford, whose brother William had bought the place. He told Mr Harford about the many happy weeks that he had spent in that home when he was a child, and he talked with him about 'the bright sisterhood'.

Hannah, the sickly child, was to outlive all her sisters. They died in steady succession: Mary in 1813; Betty (Elizabeth) in 1816; Sally (Sarah), who had been ill with dropsy, was the next to go in 1817; and Patty (Martha), who had had a liver condition, died in 1819. William Wilberforce was staying at Barley Wood at the time of Patty's death. Patty had sat up to midnight with him talking with much animation about Hannah's initial introduction to London life. That night she was taken ill, and she died a week later. Wilberforce wrote of her in his diary: 'Never was there a more generous, benevolent creature, more self-denying to herself, or kind to others.'[12]

The death of Hannah's devoted younger sister and co-worker came particularly hard since Hannah could reasonably have expected to spend her last days in Patty's company. In the last year of her life, Patty had herself distributed some 1,300 school awards to children and parents. Hannah attempted to pick up the threads of Patty's work, but she was plagued by ill health. She spent most of seven years, from 1818 to 1825, as a chronically sick person in two upstairs rooms, almost unable to bear the loneliness and the memories of the rest of the house. Hannah wanted and expected to die and rehearsed her deathbed scene on more than one occasion. But the grave eluded her for another decade, although death and illness occupied much of her thinking and correspondence.

Despite her confinement Hannah continued to receive a host of visitors. One was Mrs S.C. Hall, an aspiring writer, who visited Barley Wood on 6 January 1825, driving out from Bristol by carriage and horses in somewhat perilous conditions during a fall of sleet and snow. Mrs Hall describes her arrival:

> *At length we saw the chimneys of Barley Wood above the trees, and driving along between high hedges of evergreens, whose bright leaves occasionally pierced through masses of snow, we drew up with a frosty crash at the door of 'the schoolmaster's daughter'. It was a pretty cottage — simply and purely rustic; even in winter, it looked cheerful, with its eaves where swallows build, its covering of English thatch, and its many homely props — pillars hewn from the adjacent wood, which the axe of the woodman had not desecrated by fashioning.[13]*

At length Mrs Hall and her unnamed companion(s) were shown upstairs to a comfortable book-lined room with a warm glowing fire where a party of three ladies and a little boy sat around a table laden with cake and wine.

> *To the cake the little fellow was doing ample justice, and a diminutive old lady was in the act of adding another piece to*

*that already upon his plate; she moved to meet us — it was
the least possible movement, but it was most courteous. Instead of
black velvet, Hannah More wore a dress of very light green
silk — a white China crepe shawl was folded over her shoulders;
her white hair was frizzed, after a by-gone fashion, above her
brow, and that backed, as it were, by a very full double border
of rich lace . . . The visitor and her son soon took their leave;
'Mrs Hannah' stooped and kissed the boy, not as old maidens
usually kiss children — with a kiss of necessity — or a kiss
of compliment; she took his smiling rosy fearless face between
her hands, and looked down upon it for a moment, as a
mother would; then kissed it fondly more than once.*

The new visitors were shown around the room by Hannah's
companion, probably Mary Frowd, and they admired the various
editions and translations of Miss More's works, as well as other
treasures including David Garrick's gift of an inkstand made from
Shakespeare's mulberry tree. Mrs Hall recorded Hannah's words:

*'Yes, this place in itself is a great blessing from the hand of
Heaven, and the trees you praise are well grown, and have taken
deep root; and old as I am, there are times when I feel it
a duty to be careful lest I become too deeply rooted myself in a soil
sanctified by friends and friendships!'*

She then went on to write:

*Her voice had a pleasant tone, and her manner was quite devoid
of affectation or dictation; she spoke as one expecting a reply, and
by no means like an oracle. And those bright immortal eyes
of hers — not wearied by looking at the world for more than eighty
years, but clear and far seeing then, laughing, too, when she
spoke cheerfully . . .*

Mrs Hall's party braved the cold to examine the monuments in the
garden to Bishop Beilby Porteus and John Locke. The first was
erected by Hannah herself 'in grateful memory of long and faithful
friendship', and Locke's was erected by Mrs Montagu and given
to Hannah. On return to the warmth of the upper room, Hannah
spoke about her friendship with Wilberforce and his efforts to free
the slaves, and about old friends such as Mrs Carter, Mrs Thrale,
and Dr Johnson. She spoke with great affection of David Garrick
and of his extraordinary genius. 'Ah if HE had been alive, it would

indeed have been a trial to have retired from the world . . . I should have liked to have looked upon his face once more, but they only showed me his coffin.' Hannah then showed her visitors 'some mementos of my wicked days', including some tickets and the programme for her play *Percy*. Her visitors rose to leave more than once, 'awe having subsided into affectionate respect towards the fragile woman who had held fast to what she believed right, unflinchingly'.

The loss of her sisters meant that Hannah was left alone to bear the burden of hospitality and household management, although she was helped by the regular companionship of Mary Frowd, and long visits from two sisters, Mary and Margaret Roberts. Hannah wrote to Wilberforce in the summer of 1825:

> As to myself, I think I was never more hurried, more engaged, or more loaded with cares than at present. I do not mean afflictions, but a total want of that article for which I built my house and planted my grove, — I mean retirement; it is a thing I know only by name. I think Miss Frowd says that I saw eighty persons last week. I know not how to help it. If my guests are old, I see them out of respect; if young, I hope I may do them a little good; if they come from a distance, I feel as if I ought to see them on that account; if near home, my neighbours would be jealous of my seeing strangers, and excluding them. My levé however is from twelve to three o'clock, so that I get my mornings and evenings to myself, except now and then an old friend steals in quietly for a night or two, as the franker of this letter for example.[14]

It is perhaps not surprising in these circumstances that the management of the household ran out of control. Hannah's friends expressed alarm at the rumours of wild goings on in the servants' hall. Zachary Macaulay felt it his duty to investigate. He found evidence of theft and other misdeeds below stairs by 'eight pampered minions'. Expenditure had grossly exceeded income and it became necessary for Hannah to leave Barley Wood in 1828. 'Driven like Eve out of Paradise, but unlike Eve not by angels,'[15] was her own parting comment. Barley Wood was sold to William Harford.

17
THE HAPPY SAINT

There is no happy death
but that which conducts to a happy immortality.

Practical Piety

On 18 April 1828 Hannah More moved to the house of an old
friend, the Reverend Dr Thomas Whalley, at 4 Windsor Terrace,
Hotwells, in the parish of Clifton, Bristol. From there she wrote to
Wilberforce:

> *I am diminishing my worldly cares. I have sold Barley Wood,
> and have just parted with the copyright to Cadell, of those few of
> my writings which I had not sold him before. I have exchanged the
> eight 'pampered minions', for four sober servants. I have greatly
> lessened my house expenses, which enables me to maintain my
> schools, and enlarge my charities. My schools alone, with clothing,
> rents, &c. cost me £250, a year.*[1]

In Clifton, Hannah was attended by her faithful companion Mary
Frowd, who also supervised the running of the schools. At last
Hannah found some peace and rest. Her memory gradually faded
and she gave up her writing. But her vivacity and wit remained
until in November 1832 she suffered considerable deterioration in
her mental and physical health. Bronchitis set in followed by
a fever which gradually wasted her strength for her remaining ten
months. Her physician, Dr Carrick, who attended her over these
last years, paid a remarkable tribute to his patient:

> *So long as her intellectual faculties remained but moderately*

*impaired, her wonted cheerfulness and playfulness of disposition
did not forsake her; and at no period in her declining life did
an impatient expression escape her lips, even in moments of painful
suffering . . . To the very last her eye was not dim; she could read
with ease, and without spectacles, the smallest print. Her hearing
was almost unimpaired; and until very near the close of her life,
her features were not shrunk, nor wrinkled, nor uncomely . . . It
has been my fortune, during a long and close intercourse
with mankind, to have enjoyed many and valuable opportunities of
observing and studying the human character, under various
and trying circumstances; but never, I can say with truth, have I
known a character in all respects so perfect as that of Mrs
Hannah More.[2]*

Hannah had long prepared herself for death. She had written a
chapter in her *Practical Piety* on 'The Temper and Conduct of
Christians in Sickness and in Death'. She believed in a proper
discipline and rule of life to prepare the Christian for the trials
of sickness and dying. But for Hannah 'a gloomy stoicism is not
Christian heroism. A melancholy non-resistance is not Christian
resignation.'[3] She wrote that the sick-bed affords time for reflection
and prayer. The suffering Christian should be grateful for small
reliefs and refrain from murmurings. If inclined to wish for
recovery 'it is only that he may glorify God by his future life,
more than he has done by its past'.[4] The tendency to selfish
preoccupation with sickness must be resisted by spending time
in reviewing one's life, repenting of sin and remembering the
sufferings of Christ. Even long sleepless nights could be put to
good use.

*The night also will be made to the praying Christian a season
of heart-searching thought, and spiritual consolation. Solitude and
stillness completely shut out the world, its business, its cares, its
impertinences. The mind is sobered, the passions are stilled: it seems
to the watchful Christian, as if there were in the universe only
God and his own soul. It is an inexpressible consolation to him to
feel that the one Being in the universe, who never slumbereth
or sleepeth, is the very Being to whom he has free access, even in
the most unseasonable hours . . . If the wearied and restless body
be tempted to exclaim, 'Would God it were morning!' the very term
suggests the most consoling of all images. The quickened mind*

shoots forward beyond this vale of tears, beyond the dark valley of
the shadow of death; it stretches onward to the joyful morning of
the Resurrection; it anticipates that blessed state where there is no
more weeping and no more night; no weeping, for God's own hand
shall wipe away the tears; no night, for the Lamb himself shall
be the light.[5]

This prospect of what lies ahead brought infinite comfort and
expectation:

As he approaches the land of realities the shadows of this world
cease to interest him or mislead him. The films are removed
from his eyes. Objects are stripped of their false lustre. Nothing
that is really little any longer looks great. The mists of vanity are
dispersed . . . He has ceased to lean on the world for he has
found it both a reed and a spear; it has failed and it has pierced
him . . . But he knows in whom he has trusted, and therefore
knows not what he should fear. He looks upwards with holy but
humble confidence to that great Shepherd, who having long since
conducted him into green pastures, having by his rod corrected
and by his staff supported him, will, he humbly trusts, guide him
through the dark valley of the shadow of death, and safely land
him on the peaceful shores of everlasting rest.[6]

The occasion now arose for Hannah to prove that 'religion is not a
beautiful theory but a soul sustaining truth'.[7] Miss Frowd prayed
with her and read to her from the Prayer Book and the Bible.
Hannah frequently quoted Scripture and uttered prayer and praise
aloud. She constantly blessed those around her and hoped that they
would meet in a happier world. As Mary Frowd knelt by her bed,
Hannah said to her:

'I love you, my dear child, with fervency. It will be pleasant
to you twenty years hence to remember that I said this on my death-
bed. Be near me, and with me as much as you can, will you?
I may last out a few days — how long does the doctor think I shall
live? . . . I hope my temper is not peevish, or troublesome.' And on
being answered that it was the temper of an angel, she said,
'Oh no, not of an angel! but of a very highly-favoured servant of
the Lord, my Saviour.'[8]

Hannah died on 7 September 1833, aged eighty-eight years. She was
buried beside her sisters in Wrington churchyard. Bristol gave honour
to a famous daughter. Churches tolled their bells as the funeral

cortège passed through the streets. The local gentry and crowds of country people, mostly in dark mourning, met the procession at Barley Wood and followed in its rear. Two hundred children from her schools preceded the clergy and the coffin into the church. A flat stone with an iron railing beneath a gnarled old tree marked her final resting place.

She left an estate of thirty thousand pounds which was distributed among some seventy charities and religious societies and her schools and clubs. Some hundred friends were given bequests. They included a relative, Harriet Mills, who received £1,000, and Hannah's companion in later years, Mary Frowd, who received £1,120. Hannah bequeathed £1,000 to the Bristol Royal Infirmary and the residuary of her estate to a new church in the parish of St Philip's, Bristol. Few were forgotten or omitted except Tom Macaulay, whose bequest of books was deleted in a late codicil, perhaps when Hannah's mind was beginning to go.

Hannah More was a staunch churchwoman all her life. She approved of the national benefits brought by an established church, and applauded Anglicanism for its middle way between ritualism and austerity. She said of the Church of England, 'though her worship be wisely popular, it is also deeply spiritual; though simple it is sublime'.[9] Her convictions became of a distinctly evangelical character in her middle thirties. In identifying herself with this cause she was prepared where necessary to cross denominational lines. She was ready too to suffer the obloquy which religious enthusiasm can evince in others. And she lived to see the vindication of her own religious inclinations. 'It is,' wrote Hannah in 1825, 'a singular satisfaction to me that I have lived to see such an increase of genuine religion among the higher classes of society. Mr Wilberforce and I agree that whereas we knew one instance thirty years ago there are now a dozen or more.'[10]

She remained throughout her life a high Tory in politics. This was not because she sought to preserve privileges for herself or her class. She feared that revolution would make the plight of the poor worse and not better. Nor could she understand how altering the Constitution or the franchise would benefit the poor.

> *If Birmingham ten members had*
> *Think you the times would be less bad?*
> *That annual Parliaments would tend*
> *The price of bread or malt to mend?*

146

Distress was not the result of 'our governments and laws' but God's judgment against atheism and sedition.

> *I do believe these times were sent*
> *For warning and for punishment,*
> *Of God's displeasure they're the token*
> *Because his holy laws were broken.*[11]

The remedy for poverty lay not in equality, which would reduce all to penury, but in the greatest possible benevolence and charity by the well-off. Hannah never allowed her conservatism to stand in the way of action where practical measures of relief were at hand. This is evidenced by her campaign against the slave trade, and the support she gave the Shipham miners and the Nailsea glass-workers. But she suffered from the inability to distinguish agitation for reform from agitation for revolution. Her patronage was sincerely well-intended, but she was not capable of understanding the economic and social changes affecting the England of her day, or the desire of increasing numbers to have a say in their own government and welfare.

Her educational views were similarly short-sighted. They were appropriate enough for a static society, but unsuited to a world of industrial and social change. Nevertheless she must be given full credit for actually doing, with very limited resources, something of positive value for the religious and educational development of the children of the Mendip villages. E.M. Forster, whose great-aunt was Hannah's god-daughter, made this comment:

> *As to her work, it was good if education is good. She taught the*
> *poor to read and wash, observe Sunday and honour the King, and*
> *before her day no one had taught them anything. They had taught*
> *themselves. Her desire to meddle in their own affairs was mixed*
> *with genuine pity and affection.*[12]

As a writer Hannah More received exaggerated acclaim in her own day. She was well read, with a lively wit and excellent sense. She wrote naturally and easily, rarely having to revise what she had committed to paper. She had a real gift of using words tellingly in prose and verse. In a later day she might have made her name as a journalist or university teacher, but she was not cut out to be a dramatist, a novelist or an imaginative poet. 'She made indifferent plays and they hailed her as a dramatist; she wrote fugitive verse and they called her a poet,' says M.G. Jones,[13] but she praises her letters: 'Clear, vivid, informative, free from pose and affectation, they have a refreshing spontaneity, some wit and shrewd judgment of men and affairs.'[14] Hannah More's aims were too overtly didactic and missionary for her to write great literature. It is therefore as a communicator and as a teacher that she should be judged. And if a writer is to be judged by his or her sales, then Hannah More was undoubtedly successful.

As to her personal qualities, with herself she was thoroughly honest, and with others she was warm in praise and sparing in criticism. William Jay said of her that 'upon her lips was the law of kindness'.[15] Mrs George Cholmondley once unwittingly paid her the highest compliment when she said of Hannah:

> *I do not like her at all, in fact I detest her. She does nothing but flatter and fawn, and then she thinks ill of nobody . . . Don't you,'* she asked Fanny Burney, *'hate a person who thinks ill of nobody?'[16]*

Let Marianne Thornton, who knew her well, have the last say:

> *'She was a little hardened by contumely and criticism, a little spoilt by success.' Yet she added, 'Don't believe anything you hear that she said or did. She was a fine creature overflowing with affection and feeling and generosity.'[17]*

Notes to the Text

Shortened references have been made to titles which are quoted frequently in the notes. The list below gives the full references against their shortened forms.

Roberts — William Roberts Esq, *Memoirs of the Life and Correspondence of Mrs Hannah More* (second edition), R.B. Seeley and W. Burnside, London, 1834. This book was published in four volumes; the volume numbers in the individual notes refer to this edition.

Thompson — Henry Thompson, *Life of Hannah More with Notices of her Sisters*, Cadell, London, 1838

Mendip Annals — Arthur Roberts MA (ed.), *A Narrative of the Charitable Labours of Hannah and Martha More in their Neighbourhood. Being the Journal of Martha More* (third edition, with additional matter), James Nisbet and Co., London, 1859

Yonge — Charlotte M. Yonge, *Hannah More*, W.H. Allen & Co., London, 1888

Hopkins — Mary Alden Hopkins, *Hannah More and Her Circle*, Longmans, Green & Co., New York and Toronto, 1947

Jones — M.G. Jones, *Hannah More*, Cambridge University Press, 1952

Chapter One: The Darling Child
1. Roberts, vol. I, p. 7

2. Ibid., p. 206
3. *The Spirit of Prayer*, pp. 107-108

Chapter Two: The Young Schoolmistress

1. John Latimer, *The Annals of Bristol in the Eighteenth Century*
2. Roberts, vol. I, p. 66
3. Reginald Blount (ed.), *Mrs Montagu, Queen of the Blues*, London n.d., vol. II, p. 218
4. Hopkins, pp. 20-21
5. Forster Papers, cited Jones, pp. 14 f.
6. J. Telford (ed.), *Letters of John Wesley*, 1790, vol. VIII, p. 230

Chapter Three: The Jilted Bride

1. Hopkins, p. 62
2. Yonge, p. 9;
3. Polewhele, *Traditions and Recollections*, 1826, p. 77
4. Roberts, vol. I, pp. 15-16
5. Ibid., pp. 20-22
6. Hopkins, pp. 40-41
7. Roberts, vol. I, pp. 27-28
8. *Essays*, p. 75
9. Ibid., pp. 81-82

Chapter Four: The London Celebrity

1. Roberts, vol. I, p. 70
2. Ibid., p. 52
3. Ibid., p. 49
4. Ibid., p. 54
5. Ibid., pp. 51-52
6. Ibid., p. 222
7. Ibid., p. 54
8. Ibid., p. 65
9. Ibid., p. 66
10. Ibid., pp. 66-67
11. Ibid., pp. 251-52
12. Ibid., pp. 168-69
13. Ibid., p. 39
14. Ibid., p. 68
15. Ibid., p. 78

16. Hopkins, p. 84
17. Roberts, vol. I, p. 113
18. *Christian Morals*, vol. II, pp. 229-31
19. Roberts, vol. I, p. 72
20. Ibid., p. 56

Chapter Five: The Blue Stocking
1. Thompson, p. 25
2. Jones, p. 41
3. Roberts, vol. I, pp. 69-70
4. Ibid., p. 89
5. Ibid., pp. 94-95
6. *Essays*, pp. 2-3
7. Ibid., pp. 4-5
8. Ibid., pp. 8-9
9. Ibid., pp. 18-19
10. Ibid., pp. 33-34
11. Roberts, vol. I, p. 125
12. Ibid., p. 127
13. Ibid., pp. 133-34
14. Ibid., p. 146
15. Ibid., pp. 147-49
16. Garrick correspondence in the Folgar Shakespeare Library
17. Roberts, vol. I, p. 158
18. Hopkins, p. 88
19. Roberts, vol. I, p. 167
20. Ibid., p. 64
21. Ibid., p. 72
22. Ibid., p. 56
23. Ibid., p. 57
24. Roberts, vol. II, p. 55

Chapter Six: The Fledgling Evangelical
1. Roberts, vol. II, pp. 27-28
2. *Christian Morals*, vol. II, pp. 8-9
3. Roberts, vol. III, p. 62
4. *Christian Morals*, vol. II, pp. 1-2
5. Ibid., pp. 5-6, 12
6. Ibid., p. 38
7. Ibid., pp. 7, 34-35
8. Roberts, vol. III, p. 61

9. John Venn, *Sermons 1814-18* (3 volumes)
10. Roberts, vol. I, pp. 236-37
11. Ibid., p. 188
12. Letter from Hannah More to Mrs Bouverie, 1788, taken from Lady Chatterton, *Memorials of Admiral Gambier*, 1861, vol. I, p. 154
13. Cited by Jones
14. Roberts, vol. II, p. 116
15. Ibid., p. 38
16. Ibid., pp. 19-20
17. Ibid., pp. 83-84

Chapter Seven: The Noble Patron
1. Roberts, vol. I, p. 336
2. Ibid., pp. 368-69
3. *Poems on Various Occasions*, 1785. Four editions were published
4. Roberts, vol. I, p. 391

Chapter Eight: The Indignant Abolitionist
1. Roberts, vol. II, pp. 70-71
2. Ibid., p. 106
3. Roberts, vol. I, pp. 253-54
4. Roberts, vol. II, p. 105
5. Ibid., p. 235
6. *The Spirit of Prayer*, pp. 95-96

Chapter Nine: The Mendip Reformer
1. *Mendip Annals*, p. 13
2. Roberts, vol. II, p. 146
3. *Mendip Annals*, p. 13
4. Letter from Hannah More to Mrs Bouverie, taken from Lady Chatterton, *Memorials of Admiral Gambier*, 1861, vol. I, pp. 295-96
5. Letter from Hannah More to Mrs Bouverie and Sir Charles Middleton, taken from Lady Chatterton, op. cit., vol. I, p. 291
6. *Mendip Annals*, p. 7
7. Ibid., pp. 36-37
8. Ibid., p. 109
9. Roberts, vol. II, p. 170

10. Ibid., p. 189
11. Letter from Hannah More to Mrs Bowdler, *Mendip Annals*, pp. 6-9
12. Roberts, vol. IV, p. 176

Chapter Ten: The Greater Schools
1. Roberts, vol. II, p. 208
2. Ibid., p. 213
3. Ibid., p. 211
4. Ibid., pp. 218-19
5. *Mendip Annals*, pp. 121-24
6. Ibid., p. 79
7. W.G. Maton, *Observations relative to . . . the Western Counties of England*, Somerset 1797, vol. II
8. *Mendip Annals*, p. 28
9. Ibid., pp. 81-82
10. Roberts, vol. II, pp. 315-16
11. Roberts, vol. IV, p. 32
12. *Mendip Annals*, p. 62
13. *Clevedon Mercury and Courier*, 25 January 1958
14. *Mendip Annals*, p. 70
15. Ibid., p. 155
16. Ibid., p. 199
17. Ibid., p. 205
18. Ibid., p. 229

Chapter Eleven: The Lesser Schools
1. *Mendip Annals*, p. 71
2. Ibid., p. 197
3. Ibid., pp. 229-30
4. Roberts, vol. II, p. 209
5. *Mendip Annals*, p. 42
6. Ibid., p. 194
7. Ibid., p. 209
8. Ibid., p. 211
9. Ibid., p. 212
10. Ibid., p. 225
11. Ibid., p. 228
12. Roberts, vol. II, p. 464
13. Ibid., p. 464
14. *Mendip Annals*, p. 48

15. Ibid., p. 98
16. Ibid., p. 8
17. Ibid., p. 6
18. Roberts, II, p. 275
19. *Mendip Annals*, p. 133

Chapter Twelve: The Reluctant Controversialist
1. *Mendip Annals*, p. 167
2. Roberts, vol. II, p. 220
3. *Mendip Annals*, p. 198
4. Ibid., p. 227
5. Letter from Rev. T. Bere to Rev. Dr Crossman, 21 August 1800, taken from *The Controversy between Mrs H. More and the Curate of Blagdon*, 1801
6. Roberts, vol. III, p. 149
7. Ibid., p. 144
8. Ibid., p. 148
9. Ibid., pp. 123-40
10. Ibid., pp. 140-41
11. Ibid., p. 196

Chapter Thirteen: The Christian Moralist
1. Cited Hopkins, p. 25
2. *Strictures*, vol. I, p. ix
3. Ibid., p. 2
4. Ibid., p. 3
5. Ibid., p. 99
6. Ibid., p. 215
7. Ibid., pp. 216-17
8. Ibid., p. 219
9. *Strictures*, vol. II, p. 33
10. *Strictures*, vol. I, pp. 154-55
11. Ibid., pp. 162-63
12. Ibid., pp. 287-88
13. *Strictures*, vol. II, p. 95
14. *Strictures*, vol. I, p. 101
15. Ibid., p. 103
16. Ibid., pp. 135-36
17. Ibid., p. 142
18. *Hints*, vol. I, p. 67
19. Ibid., p. 18

20. Jones, p. 201, citing Lady Chatterton, *Memorials of Admiral Gambier*, 1861 (Preface)

Chapter Fourteen: The Popular Propagandist
1. Roberts, vol. II, p. 378
2. Henry Thompson (curate of Wrington), *Life of Hannah More*, cited in Jones, p. 145
3. Yonge, p. 122
4. Jones, p. 148
5. Roberts, vol. IV, pp. 10 f.
6. J.C. Colquhoun, *Wilberforce: His Friends and Times*, 1867, p. 122
7. D.H. Newsome, 'Fathers and Sons' in *Historical Journal*, vol. VI, 1963. *See also* Ford K. Brown, *Fathers of the Victorian Church*; and Ian Bradley, *The Call to Seriousness*
8. At the time of writing I cannot trace this quotation

Chapter Fifteen: The Spiritual Writer
1. *Christian Morals*, vol. I, pp. 18-19
2. Ibid., pp. 8-9
3. *Essays on Various Subjects*, pp. 150-51
4. Ibid., pp. 164-66
5. *Christian Morals*, vol. II, p. 111
6. *Hints Towards the Education of a Young Princess*, vol. I, p. 212
7. Ibid., p. 215
8. *Christian Morals*, vol. II, pp. 213-14
9. Ibid., p. 273
10. Ibid., pp. 324, 327
11. *The Spirit of Prayer*, pp. 81-83
12. *Moral Sketches*, pp. 252-53
13. Ibid., p. 270
14. Ibid., p. 264
15. *Christian Morals*, vol. II, p. 155
16. Ibid., pp. 194-95
17. Ibid., p. 56
18. Ibid., pp. 72-73
19. Ibid., p. 12
20. Ibid., pp. 128-29
21. Ibid., pp. 137-38
22. *Christian Morals*, vol. I, pp. 190-91

23. Ibid., p. 133
24. Ibid., p. 167
25. Ibid., p. 169
26. *The Spirit of Prayer*, pp. 74-75
27. Ibid., pp. 87, 89
28. Ibid., pp. 98-99
29. *Christian Morals*, vol. I, pp. 35-36
30. *The Spirit of Prayer*, pp. 185-86
31. Ibid., p. 199

Chapter Sixteen: The Honoured Philanthropist

1. J.S. Harford, *Recollections of Wilberforce*, 1864, Chapter 12
2. Roberts, vol. III, pp. 150-52
3. *The Spirit of Prayer*, pp. 141 ff.
4. Roberts, vol. IV, p. 296
5. Roberts, vol. III, p. 443
6. *Thirty Years' Correspondence: Jebb to Knox*, 1804, vol. I, p. 150
7. E. de Slincourt (ed.), *Letters of Dorothy and William Wordsworth 1811-20*, p. 651
8. Jones, p. 190, citing the Forster Papers, *Recollections of Miss Marianne Thornton*
9. G. Trevelyan, *The Life and Letters of Lord Macaulay*, vol. I, pp. 34-35
10. *Letters of Hannah More and Zachary Macaulay*, 1812, p. 85
11. Ibid., p. 45
12. Robert Isaac and Samuel Wilberforce, *Life of William Wilberforce*, vol. I, p. 220
13. This passage and the eyewitness accounts which follow are taken from an article by Mrs Hall entitled *Pilgrimages To English Shrines* in the *Monthly Journal*, 1848, pp. 57 ff.
14. Roberts, vol. IV, p. 274
15. Ibid, p. 317

Chapter Seventeen: The Happy Saint

1. Roberts, vol. IV, pp. 331-32
2. Ibid., pp. 340-42
3. *Practical Piety*, vol. II, p. 269
4. Ibid., p. 289
5. *The Spirit of Prayer*, pp. 207-209
6. Ibid., pp. 292-93

7. Roberts, vol. IV, p. 271
8. Ibid., pp. 343-44
9. *Hints Towards the Education of a Young Princess*, vol. II, p. 303
10. Roberts, vol. IV, p. 277
11. *Hannah More's Collected Works*, vol. X (*The Loyal Subject's Political Creed*), 1817, p. 277
12. *Nation and Athenaeum*, vol. 38, pp. 1925-26
13. Jones, pp. 228-29
14. Ibid., p. ix
15. *Autobiography*, pp. 329-47
16. *Diary and Letters of Madame d'Arblay*, vol. I, p. 188
17. Forster Papers, *Recollections of Miss Marianne Thornton*

INDEX

ADDINGTON, HILEY 84, 134
Anti-Cobbett 117
Anti-Jacobin Review 97
Axbridge 90, 91, 92, 112
BABER, MRS 75, 81, 82
Ballad of Bleeding Rock 43
Banwell 89, 94
Barley Wood 20, 38, 133, 136, 137, 138, 139, 141, 143, 145
Barrow, John 91, 92
Barry, Mrs 47
Bas Bleu 42
Bathurst, Lord and Lady 38, 65
Beadon, Dr Richard 98, 99, 137
Beattie, James 34
Beaufort, Duchess of (née Berkeley) 16, 32, 42, 64
Belmont House 7
Bere, Rev. Thomas 96, 97, 98
Berkeley, Norborne 9, 16, 32,
Bickersteth, Edward 137
Biddulph, Thomas 137
Blagdon 26, 27, 86, 95, 96, 97, 98
Blue Stockings 8, 42
Boake, Rev. 82, 90
Boscawen, Elizabeth (widow of Admiral Edward) 16, 32, 34, 42, 44, 55, 59, 64
Boswell, James 36, 49
Bouverie, Mrs Elizabeth 59, 67, 68
Burke, Edmund 21
Burke, Richard 21
Burney, Fanny 42, 49, 148
Bute, Lady Mary 42, 115, 118, 135, 143
CADELL, THOMAS 48, 143
Cadogan, Miss 50
Candidus 123
Cardiphonia 58, 59
Carrick, Dr 143
Carrol, Mrs 91, 92
Carter, Mrs 34, 42, 64, 67, 140
Chapone, Mrs 42
Charlotte, Queen 23, 24, 102, 108, 109, 113, 116, 121
Chatterton, Ann 20
Chatterton, Lady 109
Chatterton, Thomas 20, 35
Cheap Repository Tracts 12, 72, 112, 134

Cheddar 73, 74, 75, 79, 80, 81, 82, 83, 90, 95, 134
Chesterfield, Earl of 42, 44
Chew Magna 90
Cholmondley, Mrs George 148
Churchill 74, 92
Clapham Sect 12, 60, 137
Clarkson, Thomas 68, 69, 72
Clerke, Clementina 16
Cobbett, William 12, 117, 118
Coelebs 109, 134
Coleridge, Samuel Taylor 137
Collected Works 53
Congresbury 89, 90
Cottle, Amos 21, 137
Cowley, Mrs Parkhouse 49
Cowper, William 59
Cowslip Green 12, 25, 53, 55, 57, 64, 73, 75, 101, 133
Crewe, Mrs 42
Crossman, Rev. Dr 96, 98
DELANY, MRS 51
Drewitt, Rev. 91
Dryden, John 10
ELTON, SIR ABRAHAM 97
Essays on Various Subjects 46
Estimate of the Religion of the Fashionable World 61
FANTOM, THE HISTORY OF MR 114–15
Fatal Falsehood 49, 51, 52
Ferguson, James 21
Ford, John 21
Forster, E.M. 82, 147
Fortune Little 18
French Revolution 21, 76, 102, 111
Frowd, Mary 140–46
GARRICK, DAVID 7, 28, 31, 32, 34, 36, 37, 38, 41, 42, 44, 45, 49, 50, 51, 52, 53, 58, 59, 140
Garrick, Eva Maria 36
Gibbon, Edward 49, 58
Gloucester, Duchess of (née Maria Walpole, previously Lady Waldegrave) 9, 20, 44, 74, 102, 103, 134, 137
Earle Godwin 65
Grey, Dr 137
Gwatkin, Mrs Edward (née Ann Lovell) 16, 36, 44
Half a Loaf 117
HALL, MRS S.C. 139, 140

158

Hamilton, Mary 51, 58
Hampton 19, 31, 32, 36, 37, 38, 45, 51, 58
Harford, John 134
Harford, William 138, 141
Hart-Davis, Mr and Mrs 86, 134
Harvon 92
Haskins, John 86
Heard, John 27, 34, 44, 47, 48, 71, 82, 83, 115
Henderson, John 66
Hester, Harriet 66
Hill, Rowland 137
Hints Towards the Education of a Young Princess 108
Horne, Dr George 25, 26, 27, 28, 41, 60, 68
Hotwells 17, 18, 20, 65, 143
Hume, David 20, 58
INFLEXIBLE CAPTIVE, THE 41
JAY, REV. WILLIAM 60, 148
Jebb, John 137
Johnson, Dr Samuel 7, 15, 28, 31, 32, 33, 34, 35, 36, 42, 43, 44, 49, 140
Jones, Rev. 113
KAUFMANN, ANGELICA 37, 42
Kennicott, Dr 38, 59
Knox, Alexander 137
LADIES POCKET BOOK OF 1778 42
Langhorne, Dr John 25–28, 41
Leveson, Mrs 42
Linley 18,
Lintorn, Martha 17
Locke, John 104, 133, 140
Loughborough, Lord 97
Lovell, Ann *see* Gwatkin
Lyttleton, Lord 42, 48
MACAULAY, THOMAS BABINGTON 17, 113, 138, 146
Macaulay, Zachary 29, 60, 138, 141
Macaulay, Mrs Zachary (née Selina Mills) 28, 59, 60, 146
Man in the Iron Mask 65
Mansel, Dr 137
Mason, William 112, 113
Mendip Annals 11, 89
Mendip Feasts 75
Mendip Scheme 74
Mendip Schools 93, 101, 111, 135
Mendip Schools Questions, The 135
Middleton, Charles (later Lord Barham) 67–68
Mills, Harriet 146
Monboddo, Lord 28, 38, 68
Monckton, Mary 42
Montagu, Mrs Elizabeth 16, 34, 35, 39, 42, 46, 58, 59, 64, 65, 140
Morning Hymn 32

More, Elizabeth (Betty) 11, 15, 101, 134, 137, 138
More, Hannah
    children 106–107
    educational views 17, 76–77, 93, 103, 134–36, 138, 147
    influence 7–8, 12–13, 117–118
    men 23, 28, 46, 104–105
    popularity of writings 7, 12, 19, 62, 102, 108, 109, 113, 134, 147
    religion 20, 35, 39, 52, 57–62, 70–71, 76–77, 79, 98–99, 102–105, 108–109, 112, 116, 119–31, 144–45
        the Bible 39, 93, 121–22, 134–35
        charity 106–107, 126–27
        churchmanship 60, 98–99, 146
        conflicts with social life 52–53, 56–57, 59–60
        good habits 105, 126
        missions 136
        nominal religion 123–26
        prayer 72, 119, 128–29, 130, 133, 135–36
        sabbath 38–39, 62, 102
        time 107, 126–27, 128
        welfare and poverty 75, 81, 83–84, 92, 115–16
        work ethic 105–106, 122
    slavery 67–72
    social and political ideas 21, 48, 61, 74, 76–78, 86, 97, 106–108, 111–12, 114–16, 117, 146–47
    Sunday Schools 74–77, 79–94, 134–35
    women's issues 33–34, 46–47, 103–106, 109
More, Jacob, father of Hannah 8, 9, 10, 12, 16, 17, 32, 74
More, Martha (Patty) 11, 16, 24, 31, 73, 75, 79, 82, 83, 86, 87, 89, 91, 92, 95, 96, 113, 134, 138, 139
More, Mary 9, 11, 12, 15, 17, 18, 23, 42, 50, 51, 58, 59, 91, 108, 134, 136, 137, 138, 140, 141, 143, 145, 146
More, Mary Grace, mother of Hannah 9, 71, 75, 126, 133
More, Sarah (Sally) 11, 15, 16, 27, 31, 32, 34, 35, 41, 44, 113, 114, 134, 138
Moss, Dr Charles 98
NAILSEA 74, 85, 86, 87, 92, 134, 147
Newcastle Collier 117
Newton, James 12
Newton, John 28, 59, 60, 68, 92, 93, 105, 113
Newton, Thomas 20
North, Lady 48, 117
Northumberland, Earl of 47, 48
ODE TO DRAGON 45

Opie, John 24
Oroonoko 68
PAINE, TOM 111–12
Palmer, John (father and son) 18
Park Street School 8, 16, 17, 18, 19, 21, 24, 29, 31
Patient Joe 117
Peach, Samuel 20
Pepys, Samuel 56, 77, 117
Percy 47, 49, 141
Percy, Lord 48
Perry, Richard 17
Poems on Several Occasions 64
Polewhele, Richard 24
Porteus, Dr Beilby (Bishop of Chester, later of London) 35, 59, 62, 67, 111, 113, 116, 140
Portland, Duchess of 51
Powell, William 17, 18
Practical Piety 63, 143, 144
RAIKES, ROBERT 74, 118
Ramsay, Rev. James 67
Religious Tract Society 12, 113
Reynolds, Frances 23
Reynolds, Sir Joshua 7, 23, 32, 33, 34, 35, 39, 42, 44
Riot, The 95, 117
Rights of Man, The 111–12
Roberts, Mary and Margaret 141
Rowberrow 83, 92
Rutland, Duchess of 64
Ryder, Henry 137
SACRED DRAMAS 18
Sandford 89, 94
Search after Happiness, The 18, 19
Sensibility 25, 36, 126
Seward, Patience 83, 134
Sharp, Granville 69, 70, 86
Shepherd of Salisbury Plain, The 115
Sheridan, Richard 18
Sheridan, Mrs Richard (née Elizabeth Ann Linley) 18
Sheridan, Thomas 18
Sheridan, Mrs Thomas (Frances) 18
Shipham 74, 82, 83, 84, 92, 94, 112, 117, 134, 147
Siddons, Mrs 49, 134
Sir Eldred 35, 43, 44
Slave-trade 8, 16, 20, 58, 59, 60, 67–72, 73, 76, 147
Slave Trade, The 69
Smith, Sidney 109, 112
Southerne, Thomas 68
Spencer, Countess 102
Spencer, Edmund 97
Spirit of Prayer, The 55, 67, 95, 101, 119, 135

Stillingfleet, Dr Benjamin 42
Stonehouse, Rev. Dr Sir James 19, 20, 24, 32, 36, 39
Story of Sinful Sally, The 114
Strictures on the Modern System of Education 15, 103, 108, 109
TALE OF REAL WOE, A 65
Theatre Royal, Bristol 17, 18, 41, 47, 49
Thornton, Henry 113, 137, 148
Thornton, Marianne, daughter of Henry and Marianne 137–38, 148
Thornton, Marianne (née Macaulay) 17
Thoughts on the Importance of Manners 61, 102
Thrale, Mrs 42, 140
Trimmer, Sarah 74, 111
Trinity Street School 15, 16
Tucker, Josiah 20, 44, 66
Turn the Carpet 116
Turner, Edward 7, 24, 25, 43, 65
Twopenny Register 117
VESEY, MRS 42
Village Politics 112
WAITE, FLOWER 83
Waldegrave 134,
Walpole, Horace 7, 28, 42, 56, 62, 69, 76, 102
Walsingham, Mrs Boyle 59
Wedmore 91, 92
Wentworth, Lady Charlotte 102
Wesley, Charles 20, 101
Wesley, John 12, 20, 66, 111
Whalley, Rev. Dr Thomas and Mrs 134, 143
Wilberforce, William 20, 28, 58, 67, 68, 69, 71, 72, 73, 74, 79, 81, 83, 84, 96, 97, 98, 101, 103, 113, 134, 139, 140, 141, 143, 146
Williams, Mrs 33, 35
Wilmot, Mr and Mrs Henry 38
Wilson, Daniel 137
Winscombe 89, 92
Wrington 74
Women's Friendly Societies 75
Woodward, Dr 24
Wordsworth, William 137
YATTON 90, 94
Yearsley, Anne 63–65
Younge, Mr and Mrs 86, 97, 98